MW00906412

306.874
STR

**DATE DUE**

| NO 15 07 | | | |
|---|---|---|---|
| | | | |
| | | | |
| | | | |
| | | | |
| | | | |
| | | | |
| | | | |
| | | | |
| | | | |
| | | | |

**ST. IGNACE PUBLIC LIBRARY**
6 SPRING STREET
ST. IGNACE, MI 49781
(906) 643-8318

# Dad, Do You Love Mom?

Other Books by Jay Strack

*Aim High*
*Drugs and Drinking*
*Shake Off the Dust*
*The Transformer*

# Dad, Do You Love Mom?

## Jay Strack

Thomas Nelson Publishers
Nashville

*To Charles and Toni Clevinger*
*Wayne and Mavis Miller of the John Price Foundation*
*Larry and Louise Pelton*
*George and Mary Jo Sanders*
*With a grateful heart,*
*I thank you for the years*
*of love, support, wisdom, and prayers.*
*Only eternity will reveal*
*how greatly God has used you*
*in my life and in this ministry.*

# Dad, Do You Love Mom?

# Acknowledgments

I want to express my appreciation to Dr. Ed Hindson, Executive Director of the Center for Counseling and Education in St. Louis, Missouri, and Gary and Angela Hunt, youth experts from Clearwater, Florida, for their helpful advice and editorial assistance. I also want to thank my wife, Diane, for her work on this project, and I especially want to thank my daughters, Melissa and Christa, for giving me the privilege of being their dad.

Jay Strack
Dallas, Texas

# Contents

# 1

# Paradise Lost:
## *The National Divorce Epidemic*

It was a lazy spring afternoon and I chose to spend it with my daughters at the neighborhood park. As I pushed nine-year-old Christa on the swing, I mentally congratulated myself for being the "perfect father." I patted myself on the back for taking time with my children and was pleased with the picture we made of a close, loving family. Suddenly, Christa shocked me with a question.

"Dad, do you love Mom?"

I was speechless. "What do you mean, honey? Of course I love your mom. Why would you ask that?"

"Well, Daddy, you know . . . I mean . . . sometimes you can be loud. I heard you and Mom arguing last night, and you *have* been gone a lot lately."

Her words cut into my heart like a knife. Had I given my children reason to believe that I did not love their mother? I tried to reassure Christa that I loved Diane and there were many ways that I showed that love. I explained that I was away from home sometimes because of my work schedule and that disagreements and arguments were natural and normal in a relationship. I was feeling better, thinking she under-

13

stood, when she asked, "But will you ever divorce her and leave us?"

Because I had grown up in an environment of uncertainty and insecurity, I understood the meaning of her question. But I could not comprehend why she would ask it of me.

"Christa, what is it that makes you think I might leave you?" I gently asked her.

Christa began to cry. "Some of my friends at school have dads that don't live at home because their parents are divorced. My friends say they don't understand what happened because their parents used to act like they loved each other. What if you and Mom stop loving each other like they did?"

## The Nightmare of Reality

The nightmare of a broken home has become reality for many homes. Christa's question, "Dad, do you love Mom?" echoes across the land even in the most intact of families. While many children deal with the actuality of divorce, many more live in fear of future marriage breakups because of instability and tension in the home. Divorce has become the norm for children as they watch their friends' families break up and see the portrayal of single-parent homes or his-mine-and-ours marriages on television.

I am not a professional counselor, but I do know a lot about people and human nature. I have spent eighteen years speaking to parents and teenagers about how to find the real purpose of life. Every year my schedule takes me thousands of miles across the country. I have seen broken homes, devastated wives, and rebellious kids. But more than that, I personally have gone through what many kids face today.

I had a recurring dream when I was younger. I would be sitting at the kitchen table at my home in Florida and a tall, faceless, angry man would storm through the kitchen. Though I could not see his face, I could smell alcohol on his breath, and I could hear my mother's sobs from the back bedroom.

The man mutters under his breath and drunkenly fumbles with the doorknob. "Just tell me one thing, Dad," I say as he leaves. "Why don't you love Mom?"

That was a question I could have asked six fathers who walked in and out of my life before I was in high school. I was born into the prosperous home of a car salesman who had everything a man could wish for—success, a lovely wife, a son—but he also had a drinking problem. My father walked out on us when I was six years old.

I will never forget the day my father left. "I'm leaving," he said to my mother, "and I never want to see you again." I ran out onto the driveway, begging, "Please don't go; please don't go." I loved him so much, but he got into his car and left me crying in the driveway.

I was one of millions of boys and girls in this country who cry, "Lord, please send my daddy back." I used to fly to the window every time I heard a car approaching because I hoped my daddy was coming home. He never did, and as time went by I lost hope in God, fathers, and families.

## Where Have All the Fathers Gone?

I believe a special relationship exists between fathers and their children, between my girls and me. Children look to Dad as security—someone to depend on, the one who will provide and lead the way. Even though they may never verbalize this reliance, it can be seen as they look toward their father for love and acceptance. My oldest daughter explained to me one day that she seriously depends and counts on me to be there when she needs me. What I did not realize was the depth of her trust in me to meet her needs.

When Melissa was about six years old and Christa was three, our family took a trip to Walt Disney World. We had made this trip before, and, as always, we made a stop at a large mall when we arrived in Orlando. Diane and the girls headed for a children's store while I waited in the bookstore beside it. The girls were restless and Melissa asked, "Can I go wait with Daddy?"

Diane was grateful for this and took Melissa next door. "He's right down that aisle, honey," she told her and then turned with Christa to go back to the other store. About thirty minutes passed and we met together at our designated time and place.

"Where's Melissa?" Diane asked.

"Why, she was with you," I replied. I watched the horror quickly cover Diane's face.

"No," she quickly explained. "She wanted to be with you, so I brought her to the bookstore. You mean you never saw her?"

You can imagine the thoughts racing through our minds. Here in this city where thousands of tourists come daily from across the country and the world, in a large mall with many exits, our little girl had disappeared. To make matters worse, the night before we had watched a TV special about missing children. In panic I began to run through the mall, into the parking lots, looking anywhere for my little child. Diane carried Christa through the stores asking if anyone might have seen Melissa. We tried locating security, but no one was available. We prayed and kept searching.

Perhaps twenty minutes had gone by when we heard the sweetest words ever—"Would the lost parents of Melissa Strack please come to the security office? Your daughter is looking for you." We hurried to her and gathered her tightly in our arms. I did not know whether to hug her or spank her. Melissa explained that she could not see me in the bookstore so she began to walk around the mall looking for Daddy, but soon got turned around and could not remember where Mommy was.

"Oh, honey, you must have been so afraid," Diane said.

"No, Mommy, I wasn't afraid."

"Not just a little?" I asked.

"No, not even a little," she insisted.

"But Melissa, you were alone and lost," I reminded her. "I would have been very scared." I could not believe she was not frightened when we had been so terrified.

"I wasn't scared, Daddy, because I was counting on you. I knew you would come. I just waited. I was counting on you, Daddy."

The events of that day come to my mind each time I plan my days and months. A child has a right to have parents he or she can rely on through thick and thin, when they behave well and when they do not. Children have a God-given right to emotional security and a leader they can respect and trust. But in today's world, fewer children are getting to enjoy this right.

## The Battle for the Family

When I was in college I took a course in German literature and a particular story made an indelible impression on my mind. During the early Middle Ages when Germanic tribes roamed the forests and battled each other for survival, a curious custom evolved. Whenever the sentries warned of approaching enemies, the men would leave the women and children in their camp and assemble in a battle area to protect themselves and confront their enemy.

As the battle raged, if the men appeared to be losing, their wives and daughters would assemble on the hill behind them to cheer them on to victory. Some would even bare their chests as a reminder that they would suffer rape, slavery, and even death if their husbands failed. It was their way of saying, "Dad, we're counting on you!"

The family faces many enemies today—enemies more dangerous than marauding tribes because they are subtle and more difficult to see. Their attack is against the very fiber and fabric of the family; children stand to be the biggest losers. There is a melting of the men and a fading of the fathers today that may well cost everyone in future generations. God and His divine purpose of marriage has been forgotten. Marriage has been turned into an experiment in social relations instead of a commitment to divine principles.

A survey of teenagers conducted by Josh McDowell indicates that teens today are greatly concerned with the question, "Dad, do you love Mom?" Divorce is so prevalent today that many kids are dreadfully certain that, just like chicken pox, sooner or later divorce is bound to happen to them. One-fourth of American youths already live in one-parent homes.[1]

## Disintegration of the Home

Kids need only to look around them to notice what sociologists are now documenting. *The New State of Families 1984-85*, published by Family Service America, reveals that the traditional nuclear family, consisting of husband and wife at home with two or more children, now accounts for less than 10 percent of all households. The study also indicates that divorce is a primary force fueling the rise in single-parent families in addition to out-of-wedlock births and desertion by spouses. According to the study, the idea of "one partner for life" has come to an end.[2] A more recent study shows that with the current divorce rate for first marriages at 50 percent, 75 percent of divorced people remarry, and half of these remarriages occur within three years.[3] Serial marriages—multiple remarriages—have become routine.

The United States has the highest reported divorce rate in the world. Between 1965 and 1980 the divorce rate doubled. It has steadily increased until divorce has become a national epidemic. Since 1980 there have been one million new divorces each year, which to date have left fourteen million divorced women unmarried. Due to the nearly 75 percent divorce rate among those in their second marriages, many women fear remarriage.

Why are American families divorcing? Many factors have contributed to a rising divorce rate—the breakdown of religious values, the independence of the working woman, the separateness of working couples, and the disappearance of the social stigma associated with divorced persons. But perhaps the greatest contributor to high divorce rates is no-fault divorce legislation. So now when problems come into many couples' lives, it's even easier to give up and walk away from their marriages.

The legal definition of *no-fault divorce* is that it is "a type of divorce in which a marriage can be ended on a mere allegation that it has 'irretrievably' broken down or because of 'irreconcilable' differences between spouses. Fault on the part of either spouse need not be shown or proved."[4]

Think of your friends—does no-fault divorce really release each partner from blame? Do children understand "no-fault"? Richard A. Gardner, M.D., explains the reality of the situation in his book *The Parents' Book About Divorce*:

> In their fighting the parents usually blame each other for
> the difficulties between them and so it is only natural that
> when the separation does take place the child tends to think

along the lines of who was at fault. When the couple needs to resort to adversary proceedings the lawyers can be relied upon to intensify the problem of fault-finding. Lastly, the children are likely to consider the parent who has initiated the separation proceedings to be the one who was at fault.[5]

Mike Kachura, a family counselor in Lynchburg, Virginia, believes there is no such thing as a no-fault divorce. "Everybody loses," he says. "I have never seen anyone who has not come out of a divorce damaged in some way emotionally."[6]

Ann Mitchell, noted child psychologist, writes that children's feelings about divorce are manifested in truancy, clinging, withdrawal, bed wetting, aggressiveness, nightmares, and poor work at school.[7] Social psychiatrist, Melvin Goldzband, echoes Mitchell's concern. "Children always suffer more from their parents' divorce than do their parents, and it is likely that smaller children suffer more than older children."[8]

## Children of Divorce

Each child is affected differently by divorce, but all are affected in significant ways. Seventeen-year-old Susan Grobman recalls:

> Until the divorce, my feelings were limited to my own self-doubt and guilt. After the divorce, my fears took on a much greater scope. I became a classic worrier. I was extremely confused about my family's financial situation. Every problem seemed dramatic and ominous, such as the time when my father took all of my mother's credit cards away.[9]

Divorce also puts children into one-parent homes. About 43 percent of all one-parent families in 1988 were maintained by a divorced parent. Nine of every ten single-parent families in the United States are mother-child(ren) families which suffer more deprivation than other families.

Sixty percent of the children under eighteen in mother-child families live in poverty. These families are characterized by low education and high residential mobility. In short, according to author Arthur Norton, "they are a group with little equity or stature in U.S. society and yet a group with usually pressing social and economic needs involving housing, social and psychological services, work place considerations and child care, to name a few. Currently, close to one-fourth of the nation's 60 million children under 18 live with only one parent."[10]

What are the effects of this societal change? After a rash of gun-toting teens in school, educators in Florida gave their reasons for the new menace: "We have a changing society with considerably more permissiveness and lack of parental concern because too many parents are working just to survive," said Eric Whitted, a Pinellas County school superintendent. He added that the increase in divorces and one-parent households means parents have less time to pay attention to their children.[11]

Not only are society in general and children in particular affected by divorce, but extended family relationships may never be the same. Diane Mason, writing in the *St. Petersburg Times*, tells of a family wedding and the new family relationships that developed:

> My husband becomes, I suppose, a stepgrandfather, which
> probably makes me a step-half-grandmother. My daughter,
> a half-aunt to George's children. My son, a half-uncle.
> George will be my step-son-in-law. He's fifteen years older
> than Laura, and I'm nine years younger than my husband,
> so George is only two years younger than me. I ask him not

21

to call me Mom. George's sister and I decide to call ourselves step-half-sisters-in-law. And her live-in mate we call my step-half-significant other.[12]

Andrew Cherlin, an associate professor of social relations at Johns Hopkins University, believes that it will not be at all unusual for children of the twenty-first century to see parents divorce and remarry. Their common pattern will be leaving home, cohabitating, marrying, divorcing, living alone for a while, and then remarrying.[13]

This pattern of divorce and remarriage is not the best model for raising happy, well-adjusted children. Research by experts in New Zealand reveal that compared with children of stable two-parent families, children whose parents divorce show more aggressive, antisocial, and withdrawn behavior. The research also suggests that the greater the number of changes in a child's family makeup, the more problems are created for that child.[14]

## My Own Experience

Children of divorce have a difficult time. After my father left us, my mother, brother, and I went from being very comfortable to being poor. My mother worked two and three jobs at a time, trying to make ends meet. One night Mom came home and called my brother and me into the kitchen. She sat us down and with tears streaming down her face, she said, "I can't take care of both of you any more. I've got to give one of you away."

My brother eventually ended up with my grandparents, but I grew up with very little contact with him. I never had the feeling that I had a brother or anyone else to help me shoulder my feelings of guilt.

Mom and I had to move around quite often. We were always looking for a cheaper place to live that was closer to her new job. As I grew older I was struck by the same fears that plague today's kids of divorce: Will there be enough money to buy groceries this week? How will we live? Can I go to college?

I lived what are now common statistics. In the wake of a divorce, the standard of living of the ex-wife falls by 73 percent, while that of the ex-husband rises by 42 percent. Sixty percent of divorced fathers fail to support their children, and 49 percent have not seen their children in the last year.[15]

Child support, the court's answer to the problem, does not solve anything. Lenore Weitzman, an associate professor in psychology at Stanford University, cites two problems with the current system of child support: low awards and nonpayment. The average amount of child support is two hundred dollars a month for two children, much less than half of the actual costs of raising children. (Despite this low level, 53 percent of noncustodial parents are not in compliance with court orders for support.)[16]

I thought our problems would be solved when my mom married again. But that marriage did not last and neither did the others. Time after time my mom married men who were in love with alcohol. I had six stepfathers by the tenth grade.

"Will you be my new dad?" I asked each of them.

"Sure," they would all reply, but soon they were drinking at home, and they were lost to me.

Early as a child I grew to hate alcohol. It was nasty stuff, and I abhorred it as much as the bars where my stepdads hung out. One night I was waiting in the parking lot for my mom and stepdad to come out of a neighborhood bar. Mom came out alone, and she said bluntly, "Jay, if you ever want to see your stepdad again, you'd better go in there and see him now."

I ran into that dark bar and looked for the man I desperately wanted to be my father. I found him and ran to his side. "Please come home," I said softly, not wanting to embarrass him in front of the onlookers.

"I tell you what, Jay," he said, his words calculated and thoughtful. "If you'll get down on your knees right here and beg me to stay, I'll come home."

I forgot the crowd, forgot everything but the fact that I wanted a dad. I was like any other nine-year-old; I wanted a home with a mother and a father—a home like "normal" kids. I dropped to my knees and begged.

He looked at me in surprise, and he laughed—a loud, raucous, drunken laugh. All the other men laughed too, and I rose from my knees humiliated. I knew I would never ask anyone for anything again. I began to hate everyone and everything, including myself.

On one of my elementary school report cards, an exasperated teacher wrote, "If Jay would try as hard to be a good student as he does to aggravate people, he would be an 'A' student."

My life was a mess. I blamed myself for my parents' divorce because I was not enough to keep them together. As each succeeding stepfather walked into our lives and out after a season, I became more and more confirmed in my belief that I was worthless.

I hated alcohol, but on a warm September night after my first football game in seventh grade, I just could not resist the invitation to join the other guys who were breaking out a case of beer. We were celebrating and on our way to the victory dance, so I reasoned, "Why not? What does it matter?" I just didn't care anymore. I was a product of my splintered family. I had lost a brother and several fathers, so what did anything matter?

24

Years passed and I invested my life in our class motto—
"Sin, sex, booze, and fun; we're the class of '71!"

I was alone. I felt forsaken, hopeless, and unloved. I was a typical child of divorce.

## Parental Neglect: The Ultimate Abuse

Dr. Armand Nicholi, a psychiatrist at Harvard Medical School and Massachusetts General Hospital, recently spoke at the White House on the problems of today's families. He mentioned the pain and shock of divorce on children, stressing that 37 percent of the children of divorce were even more unhappy and dissatisfied five years after the divorce than they had been eighteen months after it. Time did not heal their wounds.

Today thousands of kids from intact homes feel as alone as I did. Dr. Nicholi explains that the overcommitted lifestyle of many Americans makes parents inaccessible to their children and produces the same effect as separation itself. He points out that parents in the United States spend less time with their children than in almost any nation of the world. "For decades," he comments, "fathers have devoted themselves exclusively to their occupations and activities away from home."[17] Now mothers have joined the work force in huge numbers, rendering themselves exhausted at night and burdened with domestic duties on weekends. The result? "*No one* is at home to meet the needs of lonely preschoolers and latch-key children."[18]

A mother wrote in the *New York Times* that she was concerned about the emergence of an entirely new category of professionals who spend little, if any, time with their children. "There appears to be a new form of neglect," she observes, "absence!" She also adds a graphic illustration of one working mother: "Recently my six-year-old daughter exclaimed, 'Look, Mom, Sarah has a new babysitter.' The babysitter was Sarah's mother."[19]

Dr. Nicholi stressed an undeniable link between the interruption of parent-child relationships and the escalation of psychiatric problems now surfacing in America. A new, book, *High Risk: Children Without a Conscience*, is stirring up controversy and raising the collective eyebrow of a nation. The authors, Dr. Ken Magid and Carole A. McKelvey, present the startling and sobering facts which surround the rise of psychopathic killers and criminals in society. These psychopaths, such as serial killers Ted Bundy and Charles Manson, have Antisocial Personality Disorder (APD). The cause of APD, according to Dr. Magid, is unattachment. This feeling of unattachment results from the breakup of the home and often causes the child to feel cut off from one or both parents. The child responds with anger. "At the core of the unattached is a deep-seated rage, far beyond normal anger."[20] Magid postulates that the rage of psychopaths is that born of unfulfilled needs as infants. "Incomprehensible pain is forever locked in their souls, because of the abandonment they felt as infants."[21] These bondless men, women, and children see those around them as objects, targets, stepping stones. Therefore, most of them lie, steal, and cheat without a concern about the consequences of their actions on others. They have no conscience and they feel no remorse for their behavior.[22]

The Rochas were separated several times because of the husband's drinking problems. Jason Rocha, an eighth grader, took a loaded gun to school one day. Though he was a good-looking boy with a pleasant smile, Jason pointed the gun at Scott Michael and listened to Scott cry, "Don't shoot; it's loaded." Jason stared blankly ahead and pulled the trigger. Scott slumped to the floor in a pool of blood—dead.

During his trial, Jason stared at the judge and told him, "I never intended to shoot Scott Michael, because I didn't have anything against him. And even if I did, I would never hurt anybody."

Jason, fifteen, was sentenced to twelve years in prison. Jason's divorced parents were blamed by the judge for many of the boy's problems. Two psychiatrists testified that Jason had a personality disorder resulting from a disruptive childhood in which he was separated from his mother several times.[23]

Magid and McKelvey state that young children cannot be safely out of the care of their primary caregivers for longer than a year. "Still, in courtrooms across the nation children are daily placed in visitation arrangements taking them away for too long from their primary caretakers—even to other states. This practice is breaking natural bonds that have already been established. A recent study of attachment quality among children of divorce found that the disruption in parenting had discernible effects. David Stevenson reported that parental disruption is tied to an increase in anxious attachment and is characterized by uncertainty about the continued availability of mother or father." In other words, if a child loses one parent through divorce or prolonged separation, he is going to worry about losing the other parent also.

Each year about one million children experience the divorce of their parents. Boys suffer greatly because they usually live with their mothers and have little time with a same-sex role model. Girls suffer by seeking male affirmation and love wherever they can find it. When fathers are not around, adolescent girls are more likely to become sexually promiscuous than girls whose fathers are at home. Psychologist Edward Teyber reports, "They have sex at an earlier age and with more partners, and they are more likely to marry young, to find their own marriages unsatisfying, and eventually to divorce themselves."[24]

## Where Are We Headed?

In 1947 sociologist Carle Zimmerman compared the deterioration and disintegration of various cultures with the decline of the family unit in America. The following are what Zimmerman observed as patterns of behavior that signal the end of a culture.

- Increased and rapid, easy, "causeless" divorce
- Decreased number of children, population decay, and increased public disrespect for parents and parenthood
- Elimination of the real meaning of the marriage ceremony
- Popularity of pessimistic doctrines about the early heroes
- Breaking down of most inhibitions against adultery
- Revolts of youth against parents so that parenthood became more and more difficult for those who did try to raise children
- Rapid rise and spread of juvenile delinquency
- Common acceptance of all forms of sex perversions[25]

Americans are blindly sacrificing future generations as they seek personal pleasure at the expense of family security. While some parents must work just to survive, others are overindulging in the pursuit of materialism.

Mom and Dad, do you really love each other? Have you taken a good look at your family's foundations and tested them to see if they will withstand the test of time, childrearing, adolescence, menopause, job frustrations, and the other trials that are destined to come your way? Are you willing to provide what your children really need? More money in the bank will not take the place of more love in the home.

As the family goes, so goes the nation. What sort of legacy do you want to leave with your children? A loving home is the best habitat for nurturing human beings, and a loving home is within your reach. Learning how to love and how to express that love in a meaningful way will make all the difference in your home. Whatever may have gone wrong can be corrected and whatever may be going right can be improved. With a little improvement, you can all gain a better understanding of how to make your family all you really want it to be.

One concept that becomes clear in all of the research on today's family is that becoming a *better partner* will equip you to become a *better parent*. Learning to love and accept your spouse will give your children the security they need to face the future as they grow up. In the long run, your investment of time, energy, and commitment into your marriage is the greatest gift you could ever give your children. That's what this book is all about. And in the pages that follow, you will find specific help for improving your marriage, which will also strengthen your child's self-image and sense of security. Your child should be able to answer yes to the question, "Dad, do you love Mom?" Read on to discover how you can give your child the home he or she so desperately needs.

# 2

# Through the Eyes of Children

**N**ewsweek recently reported that in Boston, Jose and Divina Masso are an oddity to their children's friends because they are still married after seven years. Jose says that their four children "can go down whole lists" of their friends' parents who are divorced or separated or living with different boyfriends. "We don't seem normal," he adds. "We tell them this is the way it *should* be; you *should* have a mommy and a daddy."[1]

How are America's children weathering the storms which assail the family? How are the children of your friends faring? How are *your* children?

A poll of the general public commissioned by Group W Westinghouse Broadcasting Company indicated that less than half of those interviewed thought that most American children were happy, well-educated, or living in a safe neighborhood. Only 53 percent believed that most children have loving parents, and parents were criticized for not disciplining their children or providing them with moral values. Most of those polled agreed that it was important for parents to spend more time with their children.[2]

*Time* magazine recently ran a cover story entitled,

"Through the Eyes of Children." Of American society, Lance Morrow writes:

> It is both the best and the worst of times for children. Their world contains powers and perspectives inconceivable to a child 50 years ago: computers; longer life expectancies; the entire planet accessible through television, satellites, air travel. But so much knowledge and choice can be chaotic and dangerous.[3]

AIDS, teenage suicide, and drug and alcohol abuse have kids scared to death. The hazards of adult life descend upon kids so early that childhood is quickly disappearing.

Thirty years ago, when you and I were growing up, "normal" families had a mother, a father, and two or more children. Though I never had what I considered to be a normal home, I still knew what one was supposed to be like. Ozzie and Harriet, Beaver Cleaver and his family, and Fred Mac-Murray and his three sons all showed me that family life was supposed to be fun, happy, and fulfilling.

But today, families with a mother, father, and children are rare. Jose and Divina Masso have a difficult time explaining to their kids why they are not "weird" for having two parents who love each other. Children from intact two-parent marriages are now in the minority. Today one million children each year face the breakup of their home. The results have been devastating to today's generation of young people.

## The Lonely Generation

Children have lost status in the world. Former Secretary of Education William Bennett recently gave a speech in which he quoted a Yankelovich study, "New Rules": "In spite of programs to improve the general condition of America's young

31

people, college board scores have seen an 88 point decline in twenty years. The birth rate of unwed mothers is up 120 percent. Motor vehicle deaths of teenagers are up 42 percent. Suicides are up 139 percent. Homicide—children killing children—is up 232 percent. The experts have overlooked the important bond between parent and child. At some point, parents began to put the raising of children at a lower priority in their lives. 'We'll demand less from you,' parents told their kids, 'and we will give less to you.'"[4]

Cute phrases such as "quality time" have abounded on the lips of people who wish to ease their guilt. "A motif of absence—moral, emotional, and physical—plays through the lives of many children now. It may be an absence of authority and limits, or of emotional commitment."[5]

Jason, an eleven-year-old child of divorce, told a reporter: "Parents should watch out about work. I know it's important since they have to pay for us to eat and stuff, but sometimes I'd rather just see my mom than eat. I mean, I'd rather be hungry than lonesome."[6]

Josh is fourteen and lives in Belmont, Massachusetts. He still remembers the night nine years ago when his parents came in and told him they were divorcing. "My sister Dana and I really liked watching the TV show "Mork and Mindy," so my parents decided to tell us right before the show so we could watch it afterward," he says. "I don't think we ever got around to watching it. I just remember crying."[7]

Josh felt alone, but as he watched as more of his friends' parents got divorced, he realized his was not the only family being torn apart. When a reporter asked Josh what his greatest worry was, he absently replied "war." But after the mention of his parents' divorce, Josh amends his answer: "Now that I think about it, war looks really small compared with that."

## Someone to Blame

Through the eyes of a child, divorce is a life-threatening disaster. Adults who have a mature perspective of time and reality frequently do not realize how divorce threatens all that a child is and knows.

At the Woods Road Elementary School in Ballston Spa, New York, a paper banana marks the spot where guidance counselor Liz McGonagle and the Banana Splits meet. The Banana Splits are children of divorce, and they are welcome to come talk with McGonagle whenever they feel the need.

Along one wall a paper mural is crowded with graffiti:

"I love my dad and I hate my mom for divorcing him."

"I got new glasses, but Mom had to pay half and she's not supposed to."

"I hate Mom's boyfriend."

"I want to live with Grandma."

Near the "wailing wall" is a patched and battered punching bag. "The bad news," 13-year-old Nichole told a reporter from *Family Circle*, "is that the punching bag gets used a lot. The good news is that it's here—and we can all take a whack at it. After you've been coming here a while, you really believe you're going to be okay."[8]

But the grieving process is slow. There are stages to the grief of children which are similar to the stages of grief through which adults must work. When the family is about to tear up, the child may experience denial or try to bargain his way into keeping the family together. *I'll be such a good kid they won't have any problems*, kids may think.

Most younger children assume they are to blame for the divorce. "Almost three-quarters of the six-year-olds we studied blame themselves for the divorce," child psychologist Neil Kalter told *USA Today*. "That is one reason they are so quiet.

They feel awful about having done such a bad thing and they don't want anyone to discover what they have done."[9]

Younger children also tend to believe that the divorce was the result of one event—one fight, misunderstanding, or argument. They are often oblivious to the pressures which have confronted the adults, and they wonder if just one wrong action on their part will destroy their remaining family relationships. They are afraid that one goof-up will ruin their lives all over again.[10]

## Fighting Back

When the family fractures, however, children may experience anger, guilt, and depression. A variety of responses may develop as their way of fighting back to survive.

Some kids withdraw from the cause of pain. *Everyone is laughing at me*, a child may think. *My family is a failure and so am I. I'll just stay away from Mom and Dad and all my friends. I can't be hurt if I don't become too close to anyone.*

Phyllis Theroux, a frequent writer for *Parents* magazine, once called a family huddle in her living room. "We need to discuss our problem," she told her children. "That's what families do."

A snort of disgust came from a wing chair. "We're not a family," replied her fifteen-year-old daughter. "We're just four people who live together because we have to. A real family has a father."[11]

Other kids choose to fight. The Banana Splits use a punching bag to work out their anger. Other children may be tempted to use their siblings or a kid at school. Divorce arouses angry, hurt feelings with which many children cannot identify, let alone describe or handle properly. Many kids walk around school with a chip on their shoulders just daring anyone to look at him and to knock it off. They are trouble just looking for a fight.

A few kids choose humor as a way out of a painful situation. These kids figure if they act happy all the time, no one will guess the problems in their home. The pain is covered up, so for a few moments at least, it does not exist. My favorite comedian, Jonathan Winters, has said that his humor stems from the pain he felt as a child when his parents divorced.

Some children and teenagers deny reality. They openly tell their friends that "Dad is just away on business." Even though their dad is a drunk, abusive, and abysmally ignores his family responsibility, to them he is still the "greatest dad in the world."

"During the grieving process," writes Dr. Grace Ketterman, "children will go through a long period which they deny their parents are getting a divorce. Even after the divorce is final, children will still hope that the parents will be able to get back together."[12]

Another way of dealing with the pain of divorce is conforming. "I'll go along with the crowd," a kid will reason. "I'll be just like everyone else. No one will know how different I feel."

## Learning to Cope

One of the most effective ways for kids to cope with divorce is through compensation. Though this approach is undesirable, it is the way many children cope with divorce. The kid who compensates will reason, "I've been hurt, but I won't go down. If I can't have a happy family, then I will be good at something else. I'll work and work until I find success and then everyone will be so busy congratulating me that they won't notice the areas where I am a failure."

The abilities to cope with divorce can be grouped according to the age of the child. Preschoolers are most likely to regress in their behaviors. A young toddler may backslide in toilet training or no longer go willingly to day care or nursery school. Dependence upon favorite toys may increase. But just because these children are not able to verbalize their feelings well does not mean they do not have strong feelings about the disruption of the home. These children are shaken to their very foundations, but they are not able to identify or put their complex feelings into words. Hence, the results of the divorce may not surface until years later.

Elementary school age children are the most open and able to show their grief. They express their fears of abandonment and rejection, and they openly try to get their parents back together.

Teenagers are profoundly affected by divorce, and they are at an age when they are able to express themselves in destructive ways. Boys express their anger and confusion by driving dangerously, drinking, and flaunting authority. Girls may also drink or use drugs and may compensate by seeking other loving "father" figures or older boyfriends. Young people will search for love until they find it, and many teenage girls believe love can only be found in premarital sexual relationships.

Teenagers also consider issues that are beyond the experience of younger children. They worry about the custodial parent's financial situation, having to get a job themselves, and being able to afford college. They worry that they will not be able to establish or maintain a healthy marriage relationship. Finally, they worry that if Mom or Dad moves away, they may have to uproot their own lives to follow one parent and leave the other behind indefinitely.

Not only do children struggle with the effects of divorce as the family splinters apart, but post-divorce stress is also incredibly damaging. Children undergo stress when their homes, schools, neighborhoods, and financial situations change, as they inevitably do. Parents try to assure their children that "all will be well just as it was, except that now your daddy will live somewhere else," but all is *not* well nor is it the same. Everything changes. Mom begins to work harder and to date and the kids find themselves totally on their own, emotionally adrift in confusion.

## Effects of Child Custody Conflicts

Custody battles must surely be hell on earth for children. Torn by their love for two parents and needing each one equally as much, children may have to choose between their parents. I believe it would be easier for a child to cut off one of his arms or legs than to choose between two parents.

If children are not given a choice, they will be placed by the court in one home and allowed visitation rights to the other. In this situation a child may be used as a pawn, a bribe, a toy, a spy, or an excuse. Never again will his home life be all it could have been in a two-parent family.

Many kids find themselves as the referee in a constant sparring match. One girl writes in *Seventeen* magazine:

My mother has been making a fuss because my dad is always late with his support checks. I'm afraid if she doesn't cut it out he'll get really mad and just disappear—like my friend Margie's father.

37

Last week my dad took me skiing. We had the best time!
But when I got home, my mom was furious. She said,
"You tell your father he has some nerve throwing money
around when he can't even pay his child support."
I hated having to tell my father what she said. He said,
"Tell her to stay out of my business." Now she's threatening
to keep him away from me unless he pays what he owes her.
I swear I'll run away!
I thought people got divorced to STOP fighting, but this
is as bad as ever, and I don't know how to stop it.[13]

If mom or dad remarries, there is an additional stress when
a blended family is approached. How does the child relate to
stepsiblings, stepparents, and stepcousins? Where does it all
end?

Unfortunately, it never ends. Many children may "get
over" the initial effects of the divorce within a few years, but
the post-effects continue for a lifetime. Who will your child
invite to his or her wedding? Where will your daughter place
her mother, father, and stepparents in the receiving line?
Questions like these have kept Ann Landers and "Dear Abby"
busy for years.

Even when custody issues are settled rather peacefully,
there are often unforseen co-custody conflicts which arise.
Schedules, vacations, holidays, and family trips often conflict
with the former mate's plans. Other conflicts may arise between new mates who must function as stepparents. Even the
most well-adjusted families often find themselves struggling
over these issues. But the children are the ones who suffer
emotionally.

The following suggestions will make co-custody work
better:

*1. Do not undermine each other's values.* Support your

former partner's right to have a set of values even if these values differ from your own.

*2. Discuss rules, regulations, and guidelines in advance with each other and come to an agreement on consequences when rules are broken.* Explain these rules and consequences to your children, emphasizing that they will be followed in both homes. Be consistent in enforcing the rules. Until compromises are made and agreements reached about discipline, children will be caught in the middle of a war zone and left with more feelings of insecurity.

*3. Respect each person's right to form new relationships.* Verbally running down your husband's new wife certainly is not going to give your children any reason to cooperate in their home.

*4. Remember, the kids did not ask for this.* In most cases, they probably had little say in the final decision. So be extra patient and very supportive of them.

## Does Time Really Heal All?

Dr. Armand Nicholi shared at the White House the results of a landmark study on divorced homes. Ninety percent of children from divorced homes suffered from an acute sense of shock when the separation occurred, including profound grieving and irrational fears. Fifty percent reported feeling rejected and abandoned, and indeed, half the fathers never came to see their children three years after the divorce. One-third of the boys and girls feared abandonment by the remaining parent, and 66 percent experienced yearning for the absent parent with an intensity that researchers described as "overwhelming." Most significantly, *37 percent of the children were even more unhappy and dissatisfied five years after the divorce than they had been at 18 months. In other words, time did not heal their wounds.*[14]

Psychologists Nicholas Long and Rex Forehand studied the social and academic adjustment of twenty adolescents whose parents had divorced and twenty whose parents were still together. The results of their study showed that children from divorced homes thought more poorly of themselves than did those from intact families. Teachers noticed a difference in the two groups too. The children whose parents frequently argued in front of them were seen by their teachers as less socially competent than their peers. They also made lower grades in school. Forehand says, "These kids learn to handle problem situations through verbal or physical aggression. That's what they think the world is like."[15]

Divorce is difficult enough for children, but often the adults who have gone through the divorce are so damaged by the experience that they are unable to be the parents and protectors their children need. Cody Clark, a school guidance counselor in Florida, was interviewed by Gary and Angela Hunt for their book, *Mom and Dad Don't Live Together Anymore*. Clark says:

> When I do see reckless behavior from the parent, like a mother insulting the father to the child or bringing out personality traits that the child has no control over and cannot understand, or venting anger and rage and revenge, it indicates that the mother truly needs help . . . It's extremely sad. The child is in a situation he cannot control. He wants to run away, leave. He may try to kill himself.[16]

A friend of mine told me about a conversation she had last week with a woman who had divorced her husband. "Even though my first husband was an atheist and the coldest man I have ever known, I would not have divorced him if I knew what I know now about what divorce does to children," the woman said. "My children will never be the same. They were hurt beyond belief, and though they live in a happy home now with two Christian parents, they suffer for my mistakes. We make the best of our situation, but I would not do it again."

## Listen to the Children

The voices of today's children are crying out for attention. "Please don't divorce" is what they are really saying. There are certainly times when divorce may become necessary because of an abusive partner or the threat of harm or danger to the child. But in many cases divorce is the result of selfishness and hard-heartedness.

Before you choose to walk away from your marriage, consider that the consequences of divorce may be greater than the consequences of staying together. In all but the worst cases, your children need you—both of you. Their security is bonded to their sense of family. And in their minds "family" usually means both a dad and a mom.

The next generation is being born today. What you decide about your own marriage could well determine what your children decide one day about theirs.

# 3

# The Teenage Security Crisis

**W**hat's wrong with today's teenagers? Thousands of American parents shake their heads in bewilderment at the statistics which regularly fill our newspapers:

- The pregnancy rate for white American teens is more than twice that of any other industrialized country;
- Twenty percent of all teenagers smoke;
- Almost 6 percent use alcohol daily;
- Nearly 500,000 a year attempt suicide.[1]

Gary Vause, a professor at Stetson University College of Law, delivered a speech to Florida educators in 1988. "This year truly could be called the year of living dangerously on many school campuses," he said. He proceeded to list statistics which affected Florida schools:

—An average of 35 guns were found each month in public schools throughout Florida in the 1987–88 school year.

—Over a seven-month-period, public school officials confiscated 848 knives, 258 guns, 103 pointed objects, 28 billy clubs, 19 sets of brass knuckles, and 32 chains.

—Ninety-two percent of all young people, ages 12 to 17 have used alcohol; 60 percent have used cocaine.[2]

The parents of teenagers are also living dangerously. The average parental marriage is likely to be at midstage when the children are adolescents. The wife is usually around forty years old, the father is slightly older, and they have been married for approximately twenty years. The parents look toward the future and know they face an "empty nest" within a decade.

It is a time of difficulty for parents. "In the case of the husband," writes John Janeway Conger, "whatever dreams he may have had of vocational or social glory have usually either been realized by age 42 or shortly thereafter, or they are not likely ever to be realized."[3]

Mothers, too, face their own identity crisis. "Similarly," Conger continues, "the wife, who may have suppressed other life goals through her involvement in child-rearing, must face the fact that her children will soon be gone. What will she do then; indeed, *who* will she be then? Both parents are likely to become increasingly aware of the fact that they have passed the height of their physical prime, and that the rest of the road slopes downhill, however gently at first. Parents' growing awareness of physical and mental aging is likely to be heightened by the obvious contrast between themselves and their adolescent young."[4]

These are years when mothers and fathers feel that love is slipping away. The kids do not seem to need the parents as much as they once did, and marriage has become a settled routine instead of a joyous partnership. There are many problems, but divorce is not the best answer.

## The End of Innocence

Of the 1.2 million children in this country who experience divorce every year, teenagers are often assumed to be the ones

43

most capable of coping with divorce, but in reality they may be the age group most threatened by the disruption of their families. Murray M. Kappelman of the University of Maryland School of Medicine believes the impact of divorce on the already "tumultuous passage" through adolescence can cause lasting psychic and social injury and the loss of innocence.[5]

Teenagers tend to act out their sense of rejection and abandonment, and so their response to divorce is often difficult to handle. They have access to automobiles, drugs, alcohol, and guns. It is difficult for two well-adjusted parents to handle a confused and distraught teenager; one devastated parent may find the challenge too great.

Judith Wallerstein's ten-year study concluded that older children are deeply troubled by divorce for years. Teenagers manifest the damaging effects of divorce the most openly. She found that 68 percent of those who were in their teens at the time of the breakup had behavior problems: the girls tended toward alcohol and drug abuse, the boys toward more serious crimes such as drug peddling and theft.[6]

According to Kappleman, adolescents depend on parental role models as they try to understand the behaviors and attitudes of each sex. Teenagers who do not have appropriate role models available at a time of sexual maturation may experience a deep sense of abandonment and become suspicious of emotional relationships.

## Need for Security

Teenagers with their wild clothes, outlandish fads, and crazy ideas need the security of a loving home more than they will admit. They need a mother and a father who will set wholesome role models and conduct themselves in a manner worthy of emulation. The example set will probably be what the children model when they have homes of their own. What will your children's homes be like if they are patterned after yours?

Because adolescence is also a time of either noisy or quiet rebellion, parents may think their teens are less affected by divorce than are the younger children. *My child is only interested in finding his own identity*, a parent may think, *and he could care less about the family identity*. But it is in this testing period that a safety net is most needed. Teenagers cannot feel secure in the identity they are trying to establish if there is nothing at home to fall back on.

When Mike was in the eighth grade, he was recovering from his parents' divorce. He and his stepfather were not close, but Mike was able to see his father every weekend. Mike's best friend, though, was his youth pastor at church. Mike confided in him, used him as a role model, and did well at home, school, and at church.

But when Mike was promoted at church from the middle school to the high school department, that close friendship deteriorated over time. The marriage of his mother and stepfather broke up, and Mike, confused and hurt, moved out of his home. He moved into a house with a younger man who was reputed to be homosexual. Months later Mike was unrecognizable. He wore his hair in a frenzy of colors and was shaven bald except for the mohawk from stem to stern. He wore leather jeans and silk blouses. His identity was totally confused. He had no role models.

Like younger children, teenagers often blame themselves for the breakup of the family. Because fighting usually accompanies the increasing pressures and tensions in an unhappy household, teenagers usually feel they are the cause of it. Often, however, they are merely the stimulus which brings out the parents' bitter hostilities. But teens do not always un-

45

derstand the underlying problems. A child may only see that Mom and Dad could not agree on how to handle his infraction of the rules, so Mom and Dad are getting a divorce.

Divorce often thrusts teenagers into responsibilities and concerns they are not mentally or socially ready to handle. Particularly if the adolescent is the oldest child in the home, he or she may be forced to take on the role of the absent parent or support the custodial parent emotionally. A twelve-year-old girl told me once, "I had to be strong for my dad so I couldn't hurt. But the divorce did hurt badly; I just couldn't show it."

## When Teens Can't Cope

What happens when a teenager can't handle pressure? They escape. Many escape permanently. When suicides among persons aged ten to twenty-four years between the years of 1925 and 1979 were analyzed, researchers concluded that adolescents and young adults who committed suicide were unsuccessful at adapting to adult roles. It was also suggested that rising suicide rates among adolescents may reflect changing family patterns. Young suicide victims showed very little evidence of being physically ill. These children frequently reported family problems, and when their families dissolved, these troubled teenagers became less sheltered and protected than before. The parents, devastated by divorce and adjustment to a new lifestyle, had little time to provide the extra nurturing needed by these troubled youngsters. Since no help came from within or outside the family, suicide was the unfortunate outcome.[7]

Researchers agree that never before in history have young people been exposed to such traumatic and rapid changes in family and social structure. And never before have young people been so ill-equipped to meet change. "Over the last 20 years there has been a steady decline in the ages of people becoming involved with drugs, alcohol, sexual activity," says Vaughn Bryant, an anthropologist at Texas A & M University. "And all these pressures have combined with insufficient and inadequate family support. More than ever today, our children first need roots to anchor them, then wings to carry them into their own lives. But that's not what some kids are getting."[8]

## Teenage Suicide

Psychiatrist J. E. Geist feels the breakdown of the family structure is a definite force in teenage suicide: "There has been more and more invasion of the family from the outside. More and more pressures are making it very hard for parents to have positive relationships with their kids. There are so many divorces, so many immature people who are marrying and having children, so many kids who are being seduced by drugs and liquor that act as a low-level anesthesia that gives them an easy way out of any responsibility. But without a strong family structure and positive models for emotional growth, we're not going to be raising people healthy enough to carry on."[9]

Mike King, who works with young people at Circle-C Ranch in Kansas City, Kansas, believes the breakdown of the traditional family is the biggest social factor affecting the climbing suicide rate today:

> Divorce and adolescent suicide have risen proportionately in the last two decades. Considering that nearly half of all marriages end in divorce, the absence of communication in the home, the number of mothers working, fathers more

committed to their careers than to their families, and the high mobility in our society, the lack of stability needed for balanced and proper development of children is not surprising.[10]

Probably the worst aspect of suicide is that it spreads like a fad among teenagers. "When one kid actually goes ahead and does the unthinkable, it's almost as if that gives permission to others to also do the unthinkable," says Dr. Samuel Klagsbrun of Four Winds Hospital in Katonah, New York.[11]

The suicide rate among teenagers is often related to the use of drugs. Alan Berman, past president of the American Association of Suicidology, points out that two-thirds of teens who commit suicide are involved with drugs or alcohol. It has been estimated that there is a teenage suicide every ninety minutes and an attempt every seventy seconds.[12]

## Turning to Materialism

Those who do not escape either through suicide or drugs face tremendous pressure. As mentioned earlier, teenagers worry about money and family finances. They are old enough to learn about mortgages and taxes, and the enormous sums of money required for living often overwhelm them.

Those fears are not without basis in fact. According to the Bureau of the Census data, more than 80 percent of the children whose parents have been divorced live with their mothers; the 1985 median income for such single-parent families with children from the age of twelve to seventeen was $15,249 (compared with $27,600 for families that had a father at the head).[13]

Susan Grobman, a seventeen-year-old child of divorce, writes of how divorce affected her:

> During ninth grade, I came to the conclusion that the divorce was actually a learning experience in a number of ways. For instance, I realized that I never wanted to end up in my mother's situation, waiting for a check every month. Throughout high school, I would try to be as financially independent as possible. To me, financial independence meant that I would no longer have to ask my mother (who couldn't afford to give me much) for money . . . Above all, I know as an adult I must become financially independent before I can ever commit myself to anyone.[14]

Teenagers of the eighties really care about money and material possessions. Parents who are unable to provide money for clothes, stereos, and cars may find that their children sacrifice needed time for study, sleep, or recreation in order to work. LaDonnia Fullmer, a seventeen-year-old high school senior in Los Altos, California, works twenty-five hours a week and earns $500 a month doing housework and babysitting. "My parents can't afford to pay for me to buy the clothes I want or to go out with friends," she said. "I wouldn't have to work if I didn't want any of those things. But I do."[15]

A 1987 survey of sixteen thousand high school seniors nationwide found that the 80 percent of students who work spend their earnings on clothing, stereo equipment, records, and movies. Five percent said they contribute most of their income to help pay family living expenses.

## Accepting the Unacceptable

Even college-age kids are vulnerable to divorce. "Going to college is a difficult time," says Donald Wertlieb, associate professor at the Eliot-Pearson Department of Child Study at Tufts University. "The added burden of divorce can mean a disastrous college experience."[16]

Older children struggle with the loss of family traditions and rituals. It is devastating for a teenager or college-age young person to realize there is no family to gather for Thanksgiving or Christmas. Other teenagers are ashamed and embarrassed. "It's embarrassing to see your father running around with a woman young enough to be your sister," they complain.

Teenagers who face the divorce of their family may wonder if the family they have known for years has been based upon a lie. "Did my father ever love my mother?" a teenager will wonder. "Or was it all an act just for my benefit?"

Dr. David A. Hamburg, who headed the Council on Adolescent Development, says there is no doubt that many teenagers are handicapped by growing up in a single-parent family. "By and large there is less opportunity for guidance and support. The weight of evidence so far is that a child who grows up with the sense that there are caring adults around does pretty well."[17]

## Caught in the Middle

Stress, including the stress that accompanies a fracturing family, hinders adolescent growth and development. "A lot of substance abuse is really self-medication for distress," reports Dr. Hamburg.[18]

I talk to hundreds of teenagers who quite literally hate their mothers or fathers. "My dad left us," I have heard kids say, "and he's living with some other woman and they are rich while my mom and I can't even afford to eat at McDonalds."

Many mothers poison their children's minds against their absent fathers. Once Marla approached me with tears streaming down her face. "I love my dad and I love my mom," she said, "but I just can't handle the way she is always cutting him down and saying that things are all his fault. He doesn't send enough child support, or he doesn't send it on time, and I just can't stand to hear my mother criticize him. If she doesn't stop, I'll run away! I swear I will!"

"My dad uses me for a spy," confessed John. "He wants to know who Mom is seeing, what she does, and how much money she makes. I can't stand his little games, but if I don't play along, he won't come to get me on weekends anymore."

"I feel bad when my dad buys me things I know my mother can't afford," said Shera. "But I like having those things too. I can't help it if Mom feels bad, but he's my dad and if he wants to spend money on me, I figure why not let him?"

Cindy's father left the family for another woman and Cindy lived for two years with her bitter and angry mother. Finally, Cindy could take it no longer, so she moved in with her dad and his girlfriend. "I know my dad shouldn't be living with her," Cindy says, "but they don't give me a hard time like my mom does. They are willing to live and let me live, but Mom spends all her time bad-mouthing my dad. I just wanted to try *anything* else."

This continuing conflict arouses bitterness and distrust between ex-spouses and their children. It is not a modern problem: In Euripides' version of the classic Greek myth *Medea*, Jason leaves Medea for a beautiful young princess. Contemplating the ultimate revenge, Medea swears, "He shall never see alive again the sons he had from me . . . this is the way to deal Jason the deepest wound."[19] Many mothers expel their bitterness against their ex-husbands by poisoning the minds of their children against the fathers. This practice, however, rarely hurts the fathers as much as it hurts the children.

## Crying for Acceptance

Stacey's parents were divorced and neither parent wanted her. So thirteen-year-old Stacey lives with her grandparents, but her peers regard her as an oddball, someone who doesn't quite fit in. At a Christmas party, Stacey bought nice Christmas presents with her own money for several of the most popular girls at school. Her hunger for acceptance and approval was so obvious it was painful to see. "Gee, thanks, Stacey," one girl said, opening her gift. "But why on earth would you buy me a present? We're not friends."

Tom's parents divorced when he was in junior high school. Tom developed a tough persona to cover the pain he felt, and in high school he tried to compensate for the hurt by becoming the most popular guy on his small-town campus. He was president of the senior class and captain of the football and basketball teams.

One day in school he felt his teacher's eyes upon him. Determined to challenge her, he turned to a buddy and clearly said, "You can just go to hell."

His teacher's eyes misted over in concern for the young man. "Tom," she asked, "Can you really wish for someone to go to hell?"

"Sure," he said flippantly. "I'll go. All my friends will be there."

He was surprised when her eyes filled with tears. "You don't have to go to hell," she explained. After the class was dismissed, this English teacher took the time to explain to a young, lonely boy how he could find the love and acceptance he had been seeking.

Love and acceptance do not automatically come if the custodial parent remarries. If anything, the problems of adjustment become worse. Research done by sociologists in New

Zealand indicate that the greater the number of changes in a child's family makeup, the more problems will occur.[20]

## Fear of the Future

Teenagers also worry if they will be able to have a successful marriage. "I've never seen a good marriage," one girl told me. "I don't know if I'll be able to say 'till death do us part' or not. I'll probably just get married and if it doesn't work out, we'll get a divorce."

That attitude is rampant among today's teenagers. Jim Smoke, who has worked with divorced adults and their children for several years, says children always come around to this question eventually. "It may be five years down the road, but kids of divorce always wonder, 'Is this going to happen to me?' "[21]

How can you expect your kids to handle pressure if you do not handle it well? The Bible tells the story of Lot, Abraham's nephew. Abraham and his servants were crowding Lot and his servants, so Abraham took Lot to the top of the hill and showed him the Jordan Valley. "Choose which way you will go," Abraham said, "and I will go the other way."

Lot chose the well-watered fields which lay before the cities of Sodom and Gomorrah. Abraham was left with the rocky soil, but he left in peace and Lot remained with good prospects, wealth, and every possibility for a prosperous future.

But Lot ignored his possibilities and flirted with the prosperity that the wicked cities could bring. He "pitched his tent toward Sodom" and invited the town leaders to dinner. Soon Lot had moved into the city and became one of the chief members of the Chamber of Commerce! His desires for material possessions and worldly regard influenced him to sell out. He had no time for God, for his family, for his wife. He became vulnerable to the fatal attractions of money, power, and success.

As you will recall from the Bible story, Lot lost his faith, his family, his future, and his fame. He could not stand up to the peer pressure that surrounded him, and his family suffered as a result. Mrs. Lot was turned into a pillar of salt because she couldn't resist one last look at her sin-ridden hometown, and Lot's two daughters tossed all virtue and morality aside for an incestuous relationship with their father who was soddenly drunk. They were only following the example set by their father.

What about *your* example? Fathers, has your son ever found a stash of pornography in your home? Does he know where you hide your booze? Does he watch you lose your temper? Mothers, has your daughter ever seen you flirt with another man? Does she have any reason to believe you are not in love with your husband?

If you give your children the heritage they deserve, you must examine your example. Do not expect your kids to rise above you without some solid guidance and help. More than anyone else, *you* are the key to their future.

# 4

# Teenage Muddles and Marriages

n their book, *Mom and Dad Don't Live Together Anymore*, Gary and Annie Hunt tell about Tommy, a child of divorce:

> Gary and I were worried when Tommy's parents divorced. Tommy was a very handsome and mature-looking teenager who immediately took up with a nineteen-year-old girl. Her family had recently divorced, too, and Tommy said they "needed each other." They certainly did need someone, but I'm not sure they needed each other! Neither had the maturity to help the other; both were hurting and confused; neither had any answers.[1]

School guidance counselors testify that each year many teenagers go through family divorces and then go blindly "looking for love." Cody Clark, a guidance counselor at a middle school in Florida, is amazed at how many junior high girls become pregnant each year without even realizing how it happened. "They just go looking for love," he says. "And they'll do whatever they need to in order to keep the love they think they've found."[2]

Many of these hurting teenagers are easy prey for child molesters. Many kids—boys and girls—are molested by men their mothers are dating. Most of them hate the experience, but they are afraid to tell their mothers for fear that "she'll hate me because she really likes this guy." These vulnerable kids know that it is wrong for someone to be touching their "private parts," but often the attention they receive from the molester is the only attention coming their way.

According to Joanne Ross Feldmeth in *Focus on the Family* magazine, "A lonely child is sometimes pathetically willing to endure abuse and even physical pain in order to keep the attention he receives from an adult who seems to care. In these cases, the child often feels he or she must 'protect' the molester."[3]

## Losing It All for Love

I cannot tell you how many times my heart has been broken as I have talked to young men and women who have sold their dignity and self-respect for what they thought was love.

Child molestation is a real and present danger, but it is more likely that teenagers who find no love at home will seek it from their peers—a boyfriend or girlfriend. Can you remember how passionate and intense was your first love? I can! One look from the girl of my dreams was enough to send me through the wall! Of course I did not have the maturity to know the strength and depth of true, tested love, but my hormones were flowing freely and hey, I was sixteen and in *love*! I thought I could find the love I missed at home in the arms of my girlfriend.

So it is no wonder that today's teenagers are rushing into each other's arms. Society has taught them that premarital sex is normal, natural, and anyone who has not lost their virginity by sixteen is some sort of freak from the Middle Ages. As *Time* magazine reports:

> Premarital sex has become positively conventional. Moreover, the sexual revolution seems to have moved from the college campus to the high school and now into the junior high and grade school. A 1982 survey conducted by Johns Hopkins Researchers John Kantner and Melvin Zelnick found that nearly one out of five 15-year-old girls admitted that she had already had intercourse, as did nearly a third of 18-year-olds and 43 percent of 17-year-olds.[4]

## The Teen Pregnancy Epidemic

With teenage sex increasing at such high rates, teenage pregnancies become an even more serious problem. The following true stories are from *Time* magazine's cover story about teenage pregnancy.

In Angela Helton's bedroom, her six-week-old son, Corey, sleeps while his mother begs her mother for permission to attend a rock concert and complains that she is not allowed to do anything. She is slowly realizing what it means to be a mother: "Last night I couldn't get my homework done," she says. "I kept feeding him and feeding him. Whenever you lay him down, he wants to get picked up. Babies are a big step. I should have thought more about it."

Michelle, a fourteen-year-old from San Francisco, is due to have her baby in three weeks and she is busily practicing her office skills. "I have to get my money together," she says. "I have to think ahead. I have to stop doing all the childish things I've done before. I used to think, ten years from now

I'll be 24. Now I think, I'll be 24, and my child will be ten."

In Minneapolis, seventeen-year-old Stephanie has collapsed on the sofa while the TV is tuned to "All My Children." In the next room her three-week-old daughter is wailing and Joey, one-and-a-half years old, is hungry too. Her first baby was an "accident," she says, and so was her second. "I'm always tired and I can't eat." Stephanie used to dream of becoming an airline stewardess, but now her goals are more realistic: "I want to pay my bills, buy groceries and have a house and furniture. I want to feel good about myself so my kids can be proud of me." It has been a long, long while, she says, "since I had a good time."[5]

Each year more than a million American teenagers will become pregnant, four out of five of them unmarried. If present trends continue, fully 40 percent of today's fourteen-year-old girls will be pregnant at least once before the age of 20.[6]

Why do teenagers get pregnant? Social workers quickly point the finger of blame at the influence of television, rock music, videos, and movies, but the breakdown of America's families is certainly responsible for many teenage pregnancies. Many girls who get pregnant have felt neglected or deprived; they have unstable and unsatisfying home lives. "Their getting pregnant has nothing to do with sex," Pat Berg, a director of a Chicago program for homeless youth, told *Time*. "It's attempting in a perverse sense to get some security and nurturing needs met . . . It's like when kids get puppies."[7]

In a 1987 *Newsweek* article, Kim Cox, a health educator in San Francisco, spoke about teenage mothers: "They're little kids with grownup problems. They're moved to sex, many of them, not by compassion or love or any of the other urges that make sense to adults, but by a need for intimacy that has gone unfulfilled by their families."[8]

Eighty percent of all first teenage pregnancies are conceived out of wedlock.[9] Fewer teenagers marry today because of pregnancy; in fact, 45 percent choose to abort their pregnancies. Five percent of teenage pregnancies result in an adoption plan for the baby, and the remainder of teenage mothers choose the difficult path of single parenthood. A very small percentage of teenage mothers marry "for the sake of the baby."

## Teenage Marriages

Shotgun weddings are a thing of the past. Because teen marriages are two to three times as likely to end in divorce, most parents today realize that a teenage marriage would only compound the problem.

But teenagers do get married and for different reasons. One-third of teenage brides are pregnant, but most teenagers who meet at the altar believe they are in love. Many are trying to make their own place in the world because they no longer feel they belong at home. They know the road ahead will be difficult and they may be financially dependent upon either the girl's or boy's parents for many years, but their love is strong and they say "we can work anything out." They think that getting by on two minimum wage salaries is easy, and it may be possible for a while. But what if there is a baby on the way? What if the young bride does not want or is not able to continue working after the baby's birth? What if he splurges their last ten dollars on a new record album when she was planning to buy baby food? There's going to be trouble!

They fully expect the rosy glow of married life to carry them through trial and trouble, but they were not counting on hunger and discomfort and real pain and a crying baby.

59

Perhaps they married to escape an unhappy home with their parents, but now they find the mess they are in is much worse.

The routine of married life settles in—getting up, cooking breakfast, taking care of the baby, leaving for work, fighting traffic, repairing the car with over one hundred thousand miles, and cleaning, cooking, cleaning, cooking, and bills, bills, bills! If the bills are paid, the taxes roll in! She nags; he yells. She cries; he becomes angry. She calls her mother every day; he begins to spend time with his buddies from high school. These newlyweds discover that life is not easy, and they simply do not have the maturity or the resources to cope with the problems that rise up to greet them.

## Teenage Divorces

When the rosy and unrealistic expectations fly in the face of daily reality, too often one or the other partner flies home to his or her parents within a year. I have seen it happen many times. When they file for divorce, they argue about child support payments and visitation schedules with all the fury of children who once agreed to share their toys but now can't play in the same sandbox.

Their short-lived marriage is over, and so are any wholesome expectations for marriage and a future. She becomes skeptical and bitter toward men; he questions the motives of every girl he meets and resents having to send part of his hard-earned paycheck to "that woman." Their child grows up with a part-time father and a distracted, angry mother.

*I should have known marriage is for the birds*, one of them may think. *If my parents can't get along, why did I ever think I could make a marriage work?*

What kind of an example are you setting for your teenager?

If your own marriage is in trouble, have you really stopped to consider the effects which may be evident in the lives of your grandchildren? Consider the next generation!

## Children's Children

My heart aches when I think about the small children who are growing up today with ill-prepared mothers. T. Berry Brazelton, a prominent pediatrician and author, has noticed that women today seem to be deliberately placing themselves at arms' length from the babies they bear. He observes, "I've had young women sitting in my office and they won't share. They don't want to get into the subject (of their babies) in depth anymore."[10] They were already guarding themselves in pregnancy from too deep an attachment because they don't want to get too close. "If you can guard yourself like that, then what kind of nurturing person are you going to be?"[11]

The story of Karen is the story of a typical teenage pregnancy. Karen realized she was pregnant, but she had dated several boys and was not really sure who fathered her child. She lived at home with her mother who did not want to face the pregnancy, so Karen called her father and his new wife to see if she could move in with them for a few months. Her dad guessed the reason. "You're pregnant?" he asked over the phone.

"Uh huh . . . right," she replied. So she moved in with her dad.

After the baby was born, Karen returned home and dropped out of school. She lived on money furnished by Aid to Families with Dependent Children, and within a year she was pregnant again.

Karen is against taking the pill for birth control because she has heard "it is bad for you." She has never realized she was greatly at risk of having a sick or low-birthweight infant because of her poor prenatal care. The infant death rate is 200 percent higher among babies born to teenagers than to those born to women in their twenties.[12]

Karen's children, however, are in great danger of becoming unattached infants. Dr. Tiffany Field, a neonatal specialist and researcher, says, "Teenage mothers are very vicissitudinary, they don't interact with their babies well. They have a flat affect, they do not stimulate their babies." Authors Magid and McKelvey say that teenage mothers are "children raising children, and they are not very good at it."[13]

Children of teenage parents tend to have lower IQ scores and they are more likely to repeat at least one school grade. "The art of mothering is not inborn," says Florence Clark, an associate professor of occupational therapy at the University of Southern California. "It's a learned process. The young women of today tend to be ill-prepared for the role of mother."[14]

Perri Klass, a fourth year student at Harvard Medical School, describes the birth of Debbie's child:

> Debbie is 16, and in labor with her first baby. After the baby is born, Debbie doesn't want to hold her. "You take her, Mom," she says. "You know what to do."
>
> "She's your baby, you know," the nurse says. "You have to learn to take care of her."
>
> "Later, OK, Mom?" Debbie says with perfect adolescent intonation.[15]

Another teenage girl told her counselor about how she felt about her baby: "Sometimes I would get so mad at him, I could have just knocked him out. But I just watched my temper with him. Sometimes I get mad and I say, 'Dang, my life is messed up. I can't take it anymore.' . . . Sometimes I just feel that way because most teenagers my age are having fun, and now I seem tied down."[16]

## Broken Homes and Broken Hearts

What can happen to these children who never feel loved or form a psychological bond of attachment? Erica Manfred, a former probation officer for Family Court in Brooklyn, New York, told authors Magid and McKelvey:

> These kids are human refuse. They are neglected by their parents almost from birth. They live in the streets and don't care if they live or die. They think they're worthless . . . and so they think nobody else is worth anything, either. They're filled with rage, and they take it out on anybody who looks at them sideways.[17]

Currently there are 1.3 million children living with 1.1 million teenage mothers. More than half of these children are living with unmarried mothers and two-thirds were born to mothers age seventeen or younger. An additional 1.6 million children under age five are living with mothers who were teenagers when they gave birth.[18]

Although 84 percent of American adults regard teenage pregnancy as a serious national problem, more than one million young girls each year are becoming teenage mothers. Like most family problems, teenage pregnancy repeats itself from generation to generation: 82 percent of girls who give birth at age 15 or younger are the daughters of teenage mothers.[19]

The reason behind America's epidemic of teenage pregnancy is an ever-worsening cycle which results in broken homes and broken hearts. Would you like to know how you can take steps to insure that your son or daughter does not experience this tragedy in his or her life? Read on—there is hope ahead!

# 5

# Fatal Attractions

As a teenager I was insecure and overweight—mad at the world and mad at myself. I was often alone. Any happy memories from my childhood were blurred in my mind, and the present seemed an endless parade of disappointment.

I was ripe for the picking by the wrong crowd. My interest in slot cars and movies gave way to following the crowd, chewing tobacco, and smoking dope. I wanted to be accepted so badly I would do anything to get attention. My mouthy, smart-aleck personality was nothing but a cover for the misery I felt inside.

"Kids will seek love until they find it," a high school guidance counselor told me recently. I found love, of a sort, and acceptance in junior high school in the guise of a football jersey. After our first game the captain of the team brought out a case of beer and began to pass it around. I honestly was shocked. "Don't you know what this stuff will do to you?" I asked, thinking of the parade of drunken stepdads which had filled and emptied my home.

"Are you afraid?" someone challenged. "Maybe you ought to go home."

Home was the *last* place I wanted to be, so I tilted back the can of beer and chugged it down. After that night, I began to drink regularly, and I conveniently forgot about all the problems I knew alcohol would bring. It didn't matter. While I was drinking, I could forget about everything else.

Alcohol was the doorway to other drugs. I smoked marijuana, took pills and hallucinogenics. Once I was so hard-up for a high that I swallowed animal tranquilizers. I was fourteen and I was a bona fide speed freak. Drugs and alcohol were a fatal attraction. If I had not found the only way out, I probably would be dead now.

People are looking for love and acceptance. Some are searching for an escape from a miserable reality. Many more feel insecure and angry with their lot in life. Unable to deal with disappointment and loneliness, they fill their lives with substitutes and succumb to the deceptive attractiveness found in alcohol, drugs, and sex.

There are no age barriers to addiction, and the tragedy is evident in the statistics. Families are being torn apart by alcoholic parents and children, by drug-using teenagers, by workaholic parents, and by the devastation that immoral sexual behavior will bring.

## Drinking Our Way to the Bottom

Alcohol is everywhere, and kids today are even more surrounded by it than I was. According to the *Statistical Bulletin* of the Metropolitan Life Insurance Company, 67 percent of the nation's adults consume alcohol regularly. In 1988 more than 40 percent of the high school seniors questioned admitted they had tried alcohol by age thirteen. The apparent per capita consumption of alcohol in the U.S. is 2.65 gallons per year.[1]

Alcoholism often begins in the early teen years. "Four-fifths of the alcoholics in our study began drinking regularly before the age of 18," notes Javad Kashani, professor of psychiatry at the University of Missouri. "The average age of starting regular alcohol use for early drinkers was 13."[2]

Alcohol has an unbelievable attraction. Now that all fifty states have made it illegal to drink under age twenty-one, underage college students have invented unusual ways of defeating the new laws. Not only are fake ID cards the rage, one enterprising individual invented "barnoculars"—double flasks disguised as binocular cases for football games. One coed at Boston College simply stuffs her bulky sweaters to look pregnant. She figures that if salesmen think she's old enough to be pregnant, she's old enough to drink legally.[3]

But most teenagers never have to resort to such tactics. It is far easier to bring alcohol from home or ask an older friend to buy it for you. I have known kids who simply go into convenience stores in pairs. While one asks a question of the cashier, the other simply steals whatever alcohol they want.

Although most of today's media is trumpeting about cocaine use, Stanley Englebardt writes that "this country's adolescents are in the midst of an even more prevasive drug epidemic—alcohol. A 1983 *Weekly Reader* survey of children ages 9 to 12 showed that almost half reported peer pressure to drink. Last year a Parent Institute for Drug Education study of 6,155 seventh-graders reported that 43 percent were already experimenting with beer and wine and 23 percent with hard liquor."[4]

Not long ago, a father summoned to the emergency room of a Connecticut hospital was told that his sixteen-year-old son had been injured in a drunk-driving accident. "Well," the father sighed in relief, "at least he wasn't using drugs."[5]

Unfortunately, that father's attitude reflects an idea that is far too prevalent in this country—that alcohol is the lesser of two evils. Both alcohol and drugs kill people, but public opinion is set against drugs and only rebukes alcohol when someone is publicly drunk or causes a tragic auto accident.

Alcohol is directly involved in at least 50 percent of road accidents, 65 percent of drowning deaths, 80 percent of deaths by fire, 22 percent of home accidents, and 4 percent of all airplane accidents. Booze figures into violent crimes as well: 65 percent of murders, 40 percent of all assaults, 35 percent of rapes, 30–50 percent of suicides, and 60 percent of reported child abuse cases. The estimated annual cost of the nation's alcoholism is forty-three billion dollars—dollars lost through the welfare system, work absenteeism, and decreasing productivity.[6]

What makes teenagers drink? Peer pressure. What makes adults drink? The same peer pressure. Adults drink socially because they think drinking is expected. Fine restaurants offer wine with meals; most social evenings include an hour of cocktails or an after-dinner drink.

*Vicki's Story*

Vicki N. began drinking as a young woman of sixteen. "It was just a bunch of us kids," she recalls. "We were from a small town and there was just nothing to do but get a case of beer and go down to the river. We would build a bonfire and sit around and drink all night."

When she was twenty-one, Vicki was introduced to a more sophisticated avenue of entertainment. Her dates took her to glitzy nightclubs, and she drank regularly every weekend and quietly during the week.

Then Vicki married a young man in the service and found herself uprooted from her home. They were transferred often, and for entertainment they spent hours at the officers' club drinking with casual friends.

By the time Vicki was thirty she realized she was an alcoholic. "I would try to stop drinking for a period of time so I could convince myself I was OK," she says. "But the harder I tried to prove that I wasn't an alcoholic, the more I wanted to drink. I got to the point where I panicked if the stores were closed and I didn't have a bottle somewhere in the house."

*Dying for a Drink*

Despite glaring statistics and testimonies like Vicki's, why is alcohol such a fatal temptation?

Arthur Trebach, a drug abuse expert and professor of justice, law, and society at American University in Washington, D.C., says, "I think in the old days we viewed alcohol as just good, clean fun: you know, 'boys will be boys and sometimes they get hurt.'"[7]

In *Dying for a Drink*, Anderson Spickard and Barbara Thompson say that senior citizens are being introduced to alcoholism in record numbers by physicians who view alcohol as medicine. "Doctors who prescribe one drink at bedtime are sending senior citizens into alcoholism at record rates. More than one grandmother has taken her first drink at the age of sixty, only to be admitted within a few years to a hospital detoxification ward by a shocked and disbelieving family."[8]

## Drugs—Playing for Keeps

Despite many well-intentioned efforts, millions of Americans use illegal drugs. According to the White House Conference for a Drug-Free America final report in June 1988, twenty-three million, or almost one in every ten Americans, used an illicit drug in May 1988. The effects of this drug use are staggering.

Drugs alter normal behavior. The use of drugs affects moods and emotions, chemically alters the brain, and causes loss of control, paranoia, reduction of inhibitions, and unprovoked anger. These effects play havoc in one's family and career.

An aspect of this fatal attraction is that the drugs of choice are perhaps the most addictive and destructive of them all. Crack has arrived and cocaine use is up, but marijuana and crank remain the favorite drugs for "recreational use." For those confused by media terminology, *crack* refers to lumps or "rocks" of 94 to 100 percent of pure cocaine. *Crank* is illegally produced methamphetamine or "speed." Since pharmaceutical use of amphetamines has been severely restricted by the Federal Government in recent years, the once popular "uppers" are being illegally manufactured.

Besides the conventional crimes involved in drug use, there are also other tragic victims. The Amtrak train wreck in 1988 was caused by a conductor of another train who was smoking marijuana; sixteen passengers died as a result. There are tens of thousands killed or maimed annually by drug-using drivers. Children are beaten, abused, or neglected by drug-using parents. Because of drug use during pregnancy, babies are born addicted or abandoned by their mothers.

Behind the glitter of "fast living" there lies a wide spectrum of extremely serious health problems. Acute problems include heart attack, stroke, and sudden death—which, in the case of some drugs such as cocaine, can occur after first-time usage. Long-lasting effects include small lesions in the heart, high blood pressure, leaks of blood vessels in the brain, bleeding and destruction of brain cells, and permanent memory loss, infertility and impotency, immune system impairment, kidney failure and pulmonary damage in the case of marijuana and free-based cocaine. Marijuana is almost four times more likely to cause cancer than regular cigarette smoking. Users of hallucinogenics like LSD or PCP are playing Russian roulette with their brains.

Illegal drug use, which is so prevalent in the workplace, endangers fellow workers, national security, public safety, company morale, and production. These are not only "assembly-line" losses. Drugs tear away at the social fabric by impairing the professions: doctors, lawyers, investment bankers, and researchers. If you are a professional using these drugs, you are blind if you cannot see you are slipping in your ability to compete, concentrate, or to contribute in a normal capacity.

Without question the mental and physical effects of this drug use on the children and future generations is frightening. Children learn to take a pill for every ill.

## What Is the Lure?

I believe kids and adults turn to alcohol and drugs for five basic reasons.

*1. Pressure.* Many young people begin drinking at an early age simply because "everyone else is doing it." Like I was, they are so desperate for acceptance that they do not have the courage to be left out of a crowd. Even adults are prone to follow the herd instinct. How many times have you asked a friend what he or she is wearing to a particular function because you don't want to be dressed oddly? No one wants to feel uncomfortable in a crowd.

My father was a man's man, but he swallowed the lie promoted by those who portray alcohol as macho. He loved liquor so much that he would take his cabin cruiser to go to

Bimini, an island off the coast of Florida, just to buy liquor by the case. Drinking was just something men were supposed to do, he thought.

2. *Escape.* Unhappy men, women, boys, and girls are looking for ways to escape the misery they experience. They look for ways to find simple pleasures that will block out their awareness of pain. Teenagers who struggle with self-acceptance; men who are undergoing stress at work; women who find the pressures of raising a family overwhelming—each of these groups may consider alcohol or drugs as a means of escape.

3. *Availability.* Alcohol and drugs are everywhere. It is easily available in your grocery store, in the drugstore, and at the corner convenience mart. You can buy a beer at your favorite pizza place or in the most elegant restaurant in town. On television, glamourous stars greet each other with tiny puckered kisses and then graciously ask, "And what are you drinking tonight?" Isn't that how real America lives?

4. *Curiosity.* An Arizona-based drug education program, *Do It Now*, recently reported that 70 percent of drug-using teenagers across the nation listed curiosity as the main reason they began to take drugs.[9] Kids drink because it seems to be so cool and so much fun. They want to know what it is they are missing.

5. *Emptiness.* A person who feels empty does not know who he is, why he is there, or where he is going. He lacks purpose, direction, and goals. I meet empty people every week. They are constantly seeking for answers, for some new experience which will fill the void in their lives. Alcohol and

drugs will not fill their emptiness, but they turn to these substitutes only to find they do not help.

## Families of the Chemically Dependent

Whole families are affected by drug and alcohol dependence. It is estimated that every person who is chemically dependent affects at least four people. In the United States, this means that at least forty million angry, anxious, and guilt-ridden adults and children are spending much of their energy trying to cope with the bizarre and manipulative behavior of an alcoholic or drug user.[10]

Only one in seven alcoholics ever seeks treatment for his or her condition. Many refuse to acknowledge the problem by clinging to the following myths:

*Alcoholics are bums who can't hold a job.* Only about 4 percent of alcoholics fit the stereotype. Most are average men and women who are often employed full-time.

*Alcoholics drink all day. I can wait until after work.* Drinking patterns vary. Many alcoholics confine their drinking to weekday evenings or weekends or both. Others can go on the wagon for extended periods.

*Alcoholics can't hold their liquor.* Alcoholism is an addictive process; getting drunk requires more liquor each time. The man or woman who can "drink anyone under the table" shows an abnormally increased tolerance level. This is usually a sign of developing addiction.[11]

Psychologists have identified five common roles which are usually filled by the family of a chemically dependent person. The spouse is often the "chief enabler," the person who covers up and excuses the behavior of the addict. This person is deceived, but tries to keep the family functioning as if everything is normal.

The oldest child is usually the "family hero." This kid always does what is right, helps out at home, and overachieves at school to show the world that the family must be fine to have produced such an excellent child.

The "scapegoat," or problem child, is the role given to the child whose function is to act out the family pain. When he is in trouble, he willingly takes the blame for the family problems in order to avoid exposing the real problems at home. He figures negative attention is better than no attention at all.

The "lost child" is the one who simply fades into the woodwork, never giving anyone trouble. He or she is quiet, rarely in trouble, but rarely contributing to the family. This child simply adjusts passively. He prefers to be left alone and unnoticed.

The "mascot," or family clown, believes it is his or her duty to keep everyone jolly and happy. The greater the pressure in the home, the greater grow the clown's antics. He or she is the servant, doing whatever pleases the family members or "anything to keep everyone happy." Unfortunately, most mascots never feel free to outgrow this role.[12]

"With one parent unpredictable and the other emotionally paralyzed, children learn that their parents cannot meet their needs," say Spickard and Thompson. "They cannot rely on their parents and are forced to rely on themselves. They can only guess what 'normal' parents are like or what parents are supposed to do."[13]

The fatal attractions of drugs and alcohol not only destroy individual lives, but they destroy families for generations. Adult children of alcoholics face deep psychological difficulties and are at risk for the development of addiction or emotional collapse.

Psychologist, Janet Geringer Woititz, has outlined thirteen traits that most children from alcoholic households experience

Adult children of alcoholics:

1. Guess what normal behavior is;
2. Have difficulty following a project from beginning to end;
3. Lie when it would be just as easy to tell the truth;
4. Judge themselves without mercy;
5. Have difficulty having fun;
6. Take themselves very seriously;
7. Have difficulty with intimate relationships;
8. Overreact to changes over which they have no control;
9. Constantly seek approval and affirmation;
10. Feel that they are different from other people;
11. Are super-responsible or super-irresponsible;
12. Are extremely loyal, even in the face of evidence that the loyalty is undeserved;
13. Tend to lock themselves into a course of action without giving consideration to the consequences.

to some degree. These symptoms, she says, can cause lifelong problems:[14]

The average family with a chemically-dependent member waits seven years after the evidence of addiction is indisputable to admit that there is a problem in the home. They then wait another two years before seeking help.[15] If someone in your home is dependent upon alcohol or another drug, do not wait another minute to get help. "Compassion," says the Reverend Joseph Kellerman, "is bearing with or suffering with a person, not suffering because of the unwillingness of the other person to suffer." Do not allow anyone in your family to suffer alone. Get help.

## Where to Turn for Help

The programs cited in this section are just a few examples of programs that may be a help to you. This list is by no means complete.

*Your local church.* Because I believe that alcohol and drug abuse are symptoms of a deeper problem, I would encourage you to set up a meeting with a minister as the first step.

*RAPHA.* In my opinion this is one of the finest adult and adolescent treatment programs in the country. These are distinctly Christian therapy centers for psychiatric and substance abuse problems. At the time this book was written, there were thirteen care units across the country. Call this toll free number for more information, counseling, evaluation, and referrals: 1-800-782-2550.

*PRIDE.* This is a national nonprofit organization that provides information on drug prevention education for parents and teens. Address: 100 Edgewood Avenue, Suite 1002, Atlanta, GA 30303.

*Adult Children of Alcoholics.* Call 213/534-1815 for information on ACA meetings in your area or write to their central office: Central Service Board, P.O. Box 3216, Torrance, CA 90505.

*AL-ANON Family Group.* This group works with families and friends involved with alcoholics. Call 212/302-7240 or write P.O. Box 862, Midtown Station, New York, NY 10018 for more information.

*Alcoholics Anonymous.* Call 212/473-6200 for more information or check local listings. Address: P.O. Box 459, Grand Central Station, New York, NY 10163.

*Mother's Against Drunk Driving (MADD).* Call 817/268-6233 for more information or check local listings. Address: 669 Airport Freeway, Suite 310, Hurst, TX 76053.

*Narcotics Anonymous.* Call 818/780-3951 for more information. Address: P.O. Box 9999, Van Nuys, CA 91409.

*Tough Love.* Tough Love promotes self-help for parents and children, emphasizing cooperation, personal initiative, avoidance of blame and action.

Many adults still have the sins of their youth controlling their lives today. It is not uncommon for young professionals to smoke marijuana or to snort cocaine. It may not be long until successive generations of alcohol- and drug-dependent Americans are produced.

## The Idols of Success

Chemical substances are not the only "fatal attractions" which threaten the family. Are you addicted to achieving the ever-elusive goal of success in your chosen career? Is your spouse a workaholic?

It is quite easy to be overcome by the drive for success, especially for Americans—we are overcomers. History reflects the drive and determination of people who arrived in this rugged land and literally carved out a place for themselves and for their families. As a fledgling nation, they fought wars against superpowers and won. They faced hardships and turmoil from within and without and somehow the nation persevered. Americans are proud of their heritage and their collective ability to survive and succeed against all odds.

Americans idealize success. Four versions of Rocky Balboa's bout against invincible odds have earned millions of dollars for Sylvester Stallone, a man wise enough to understand this country's fascination with success. For two weeks every four years during the Olympics, people are glued to their television sets urging America to "bring home the gold." Many of those who earn silver erupt into bitter tears. They consider themselves losers. Is the second-best athlete in the world a loser?

Americans want success and all it brings. For some, the ultimate success is earning money. "I'll know I'm rich when I stop working for money and my money begins working for me," one man told me. The thirst for money is never quenched.

Other people consider themselves successful if they win recognition from their peers. For others, success is simply raising healthy, well-adjusted children. For a large segment of society, success is not an end goal. It is a process, a series of accomplishments with one high quickly forgotten in the pursuit of yet another accomplishment, another award, another project. "The toughest thing about success is that you've got to keep on being a success," said Irving Berlin.[16]

"The drive for success is back in style again," says Chicago executive recruiter Allan Cox. Cox has noticed that many executives feel a power rush from working at least sixty hours per week: "It's the thrill of the chase, keeping the score card, the feeling of having influence and power and being able to guide those under them."[17]

But yesterday's success is nothing but tomorrow's memory. Men and women who are addicted to success often forfeit happy homes and stable marriages for a series of moments which fade quickly and are of no lasting significance. Liv Ullman, a famous actress, once warned that "the best thing that can come with success is the knowledge that it is nothing to long for."[18]

Zig Ziglar, one of America's leading motivational speakers, reminds us that making money while destroying our families in the pursuit of dollars is one of life's greatest tragedies:

> If I should go to the top in my profession, become the best in the world at what I do, and then have one or more of my four children come up to me and say, "You know, Dad, I sure wish you had saved a little time for me when I was growing up. Maybe if you had given me some of the advice you so freely give to others, my own life would not have been the disaster it turned out to be"—I can assure you it would break my heart.[19]

There is a striking parallel between people addicted to success and those who are chemically dependent. G. Douglas Talbott, M.D., has described the "de-peoplizing" of an alcoholic who is committed first and foremost to his bottle; the process is the same for a man or woman addicted to the drive for success. Imagine, if you will, a person stripping layers off his life as easily as he strips the layers of an onion. First goes involvement in his church. Second goes his activity in the community. Third goes time spent with friends, hobbies, and leisure-time activities. Fourth goes his relationship with peers, people at work, and neighbors. Fifth goes his extended family, and finally, his nuclear family. At last the addict finds himself totally alone.[20]

## The Kids Pay the Price

All addictions cost the addict in terms of leisure, health, and marriage, but it is the children of addicts who pay the higher price. Earl Grollman and Gerri Sweder interviewed over one thousand children for their book, *The Working Parent Dilemma*. Listen to a few comments these kids made:

"My father works all the time," says fourteen-year-old Kathy. "He leaves home around seven A.M. and doesn't come home until seven P.M. By then we've eaten, and he eats by himself, mostly in front of the TV. Even on weekends he goes in to the office."

A high school junior remarks, "Everyone thinks my mom is terrific because she's smart and works hard and is famous. She has time to travel all over giving talks. The only person she has no time for is me."

Jimmy, thirteen, says, "On Tuesdays my parents play tennis. On Thursday they have dinner with friends. Then they go out every weekend. I think they'd rather be out than be home with us."[21]

Those who are addicted to success, like those who are addicted to drugs, find that they ultimately lose themselves. In an article in *Esquire*, Phillip Moffitt talked with a friend who is a former AT&T executive. The man freely told Moffitt that self-esteem is getting too tied up in demonstrable success. He admitted that he had sacrificed his own personal well-being and family life to reach the top. When he got to the top, he was assigned a driver and a private limo, only to discover that the driver refused to talk to him because he found him too boring.[22]

Are you throwing away happiness with both hands so you can find that elusive quality the world calls success? The drive for success, untempered and unchecked, can be as suicidal an addiction as alcoholism. Success, with its perks and

80

material advantages, is a fatal attraction that can kill families and marriages.

Dr. Steven Berglas runs the Executive Stress Clinic in Boston, a treatment center for people who "hit the bottom when they reach the top." He calls the "success syndrome" a condition that develops when the rewards of success—wealth, fame, prestige, power—expose an individual to expectations and psychological stress that make him vulnerable to depression, drug abuse, self-inflicted failure, and even suicide. "The cruel paradox of this syndrome is that at the very moment a successful person should be enjoying the fruits of his labor, he becomes susceptible to distress he would not have been exposed to if he were not successful."

"A lot of yuppies are hitting bottom when they reach the top because of their myopic focus on material rewards," he adds. If people do not realize that relationships count more than the balance in their checkbooks, they are in trouble.

When people give up a family in pursuit of professional success, they are likely candidates for a breakdown. You cannot snuggle up to success in your old age.

"The hardest thing for someone suffering from this syndrome is to acknowledge his obsession with success and what it can buy, and then let it go," Berglas observes. Then, he adds, "There is a human need to achieve, to demonstrate competence, to prove one's worth—and there is also a need to relate to people, to receive and to give love. The genuinely successful person has developed the capacity to achieve a balance."[23]

Too often people are so caught up in what they think is urgent at the moment that they forget what is really important.

Urgent things like a flat tire or a ringing telephone demand instant action. Important things require careful, thoughtful attention.

Urgent things clamor loudly. Important things are often quiet and unobtrusive.

Urgent things are many. Important things are few.

Urgent things are resolved and soon forgotten. Important things are eternal.

What is really important in your home? Your three o'clock meeting or your confused teenager? You need to be reminded that urgent things often rob you of a proper perspective. They crowd in on your days like unwelcome guests and steal your lifetime by demanding your attention for hot air issues.

## Sexual Addiction

There is another fatal attraction. Sexual addiction can be just as enslaving as alcohol or drugs. Those who are caught in a web of sexual promiscuity or homosexuality often feel helpless to deliver themselves.

Eli Coleman, a pioneer in the field of sexual addiction, says there's no question that sexual addiction exists, and that his patients include men who are "masturbating 10 to 15 times a day resulting in physical injury, hiring prostitutes on a daily basis, (or having) multiple anonymous sexual encounters without any regard to risk of health or commitments to family or relationships."[24]

*People* magazine recently ran a story on Carole Mallory, a former model who confesses an addiction to sex. "I was a sex addict," she told a reporter. "I was addicted to movie stars. Hollywood is one big mattress."[25]

Like all addictions, Mallory's sexual habits became degrading and destructive. She was used like a toy for one-night stands. "I thought attention was love. I thought by being on a star's arm, I would be famous." Instead, "I felt increasingly worse about myself. My alcoholism and use escalated."[26]

The notion of sexual addiction has become increasingly popular and support groups modeled after Alcoholics Anonymous (AA) have sprung up for sexual addicts. But sociologists Martin P. Levine and Richard Troiden wrote in the August 1988 issue of the *Journal of Sex Research* that the sex addict theory amounts to "transforming sin into sickness." Says Levine: "There's no such disease as sexual addiction or sexual compulsion. It doesn't exist. You can't be addicted to sex. Addiction is a physiological dependency on a substance."[27]

In the winter of 1987–88, *Fatal Attraction*, starring Michael Douglas and Glenn Close, was the hottest movie in the theaters. It stunned audiences as it portrayed a relatively innocent person drawn into disastrous consequences by the excitement of a sexual attraction. In many ways it was a social commentary and indictment on today's society. Wives took their husbands to see it, elbowing them as if to say, "This is what may happen if you even *think* about fooling around." Men who had never thought about the consequences of adultery began to think seriously about AIDS, psychopaths, and the consequences of sin. But *Fatal Attraction* not withstanding, recent research indicates that over 50 percent of married women and over 70 percent of married men will be unfaithful at least once.[28]

Billy Graham stunned the large crowd attending the 1988 meeting of the National Religious Broadcasters when he revealed extremely damaging information about a pastors' convention at a large hotel. He proclaimed that a spokesman for the hotel stated that 75 percent of the rooms occupied by Bible-believing pastors turned on R- and X-rated movies. No other group—lawyers, doctors, morticians, politicians, educators—used the "pay for sex" channels as much as these pastors or their families.[29]

*The New Obscenity*

Sex is not addictive in the chemical sense, but psychologist Eli Coleman says "these behavior patterns are pathological, self-defeating." He adds that the sex addiction-compulsion concept "appeals to most Americans because . . . if you're engaging in behavior that traditionally has been defined as sin, transforming it into a disease absolves you of any moral failing."[30]

William Lee Wilbanks calls the four words, "I can't help myself," the new obscenity. "This philosophy sees man as an organism being acted upon by biological and social forces, rather than as an agent with a free will. It views offenders not as sinful or criminal but as 'sick.' By ignoring the idea that people face temptations that can—and should—be restricted, it denies the very quality that separates us from the animals."[31]

We are certainly seeing more sexual immorality today, but it has been around since sin was introduced into the world. The Babylonians drowned adulterers and the ancient Greeks and Romans also sentenced women adulterers to death while men got off with a light sentence. In colonial America the accused were either whipped, branded, or forced to wear symbols like Hester Prynne's letter A of *The Scarlet Letter*.[32]

Today adultery is grounds for divorce in every state, but many spouses choose to forgive although they find it difficult to forget. Attempts at reconciliation often fail because basic trust has been destroyed; the lure of sexual promiscuity is exciting and attractive. Dr. David Viscott, a psychiatrist and host of ABC Talkradio Network, says that "having an affair consumes you and focuses you. It has the same effect Samuel Johnson ascribed to a hanging. Johnson said, 'When a man knows he is to be hanged in a fortnight, it concentrates his mind wonderfully.'"[33]

Interestingly, it would appear that men who strive for success avoid sexual involvements outside marriage. Warren Bennis and Burt Nanus surveyed the chief executive officers of Fortune 500 companies and found that ninety percent of those responding said they had a "stable marriage."[34] While it may be that many of these men battle with success addiction, they know enough to realize that extramarital involvements are distracting to that pursuit. Still others suffer from both addictions.

Why is sexual promiscuity attractive? It's exciting. It has the allure of the forbidden. It's pleasurable. One bisexual man told Dr. Viscott that he had been with thousands of men and women. What did it mean to him? "It meant I was attractive." But sexual promiscuity also is destructive.

Today as never before those who cannot control their sexual appetites are destroying their lives. AIDS has entered the scene, and it kills many who indulge in illicit sex as well as those who are innocent of sexual immorality. Although AIDS can kill the body, sexual immorality can kill a marriage, a friendship, and a relationship. I cannot count the times when wives have told me, "I want to take my husband back, but I feel I could never trust him again."

Other husbands exclaim, "We were once best friends with that couple, but then I learned my wife was having an affair with him. Just imagine! We have spent nearly every weekend together playing cards, and all the time something horrible had been going on. I can't face any one of the three of them."

"I used to love my dad," a teenager told me. "But then I saw him with his girlfriend. I still want to love him, but he did an awful thing to my mother and I don't think I can forgive him. I know I can't forget."

### Stop Before You Get Started
Whether the situation arises from lust or loneliness, sexual addiction begins in the mind before it leads to physical activ-

ity. Men usually battle with impulsive lust while women battle with selective lust. Men are more vulnerable to lust of the eyes as they seek physical pleasure; women are vulnerable to temptation because they seek emotional pleasure. Whether she craves his attention or he craves her body, the results are usually the same—extramarital affairs lead to hurt, bitterness, and anguish.

It is not flattering that a man is willing to use a woman. Men will line up to the next city to use a woman. I have always been amazed that so many ladies have their heads turned because someone at the office, a friend, or a neighbor begins to notice them.

There are times when it looks as though the grass is greener in the yard next door, but take it from someone who used to mow lawns for a living—Erma Bombeck had it right: If the grass is greener, it's usually over a septic tank.

Anyone can fall into adultery or homosexuality innocently or deliberately. But once the activity is started, it gets out of control quickly. J. Allen Peterson, a noted author and counselor, summarized the process like this: "Our minds feed the fantasy, the fantasy creates the emotions, and the emotions scream for the actual experience."[35]

Daniel Dolesh and Sherelynn Lehman have pinpointed three main causes of extramarital affairs.[36] Do any of these apply to your marriage?

*Loneliness.* When husbands and wives begin to take each other for granted and seldom speak about more than the house and the kids, they may often be lonely for social and emotional intimacy. When a lonely husband or wife finds a close friend in another man or woman, the stage is set for an extramarital affair.

*Monotony.* After several years in a marriage, the passion

86

cools and routines become ruts. Children have arrived on the scene and family life is typically monotonous. So the lure of excitement offered by an affair becomes more enticing.

*Failure to communicate.* When couples begin to squabble more than they talk or when she nags and he clams up, the walls go up and true intimacy is impossible.

As I looked out of a window the other day, I noticed that the trees were beginning to show the first blush of approaching autumn. *Soon those trees will be leafless*, I thought, *and will seem utterly dead.*

Your marriage may seem like a winter tree. You have gone from the bloom of spring to the sheltering shade and fulness of summer, but something happened and your marriage did not survive the transition of fall. You may wonder if there is any life left in your leafless marriage.

There is! Just as God awakens the sap within the trees and brings the bloom again in the spring, your marriage can once again bud forth in new joy, and your children will share in the blessings too. Although change does not come easily, you can begin by deciding that you really want to change for the better.

# 6

# Throw Mama from the Train

Each spring as the mountain snows thawed in the Swiss Alps, pounds of decaying leaves, twigs, and other rubble would flow into the streams which rose from the crystal mountain springs. It was the humble job of the "keepers of the springs" to clear all the rubble and blockage from the streams.

The streams continued flowing down the mountains and ultimately fed a beautiful lake. Everyone enjoyed the beauty of the lake. Lovely swans glided along in the pure waters and children splashed along the shore. The lake was crystal pure and clean, a thing of beauty and delight.

However, over the years the keepers of the springs were ridiculed for having such menial jobs. In time, the keepers began to seek more education to better themselves. They took other jobs and the streams were neglected. Sure, there were a few wise old men who refused to give up the job, but when they died the streams flowed downstream and no one gave any thought to their condition.

As time passed, the lake became polluted and a film of scum covered the lake. No longer did the swans glide across its surface, and no children splashed along its shoreline. Instead, the lake was deserted and ugly. Only when their beautiful lake became an eyesore did the people realize the significance of the keepers of the springs. How important their work had been! It would take many years to undo the damage done by a few seasons of neglect.

## Keepers of the Springs

Mothers are the "keepers of the springs." They guard the purity of the home and the children. If mothers become intimidated into thinking that their work is unimportant, the results will be harmful, not only to the family, but to the entire nation.

There is no more important job than keeping the home. I am saddened every time I see the role of mothers disparaged in our society, but it can be seen everywhere. Television mothers do not find fulfillment in their homes; they have careers, dating lives, and therapists. How many mothers do you know who regularly spend time with their children?

Today's economy has made it necessary for many women to work, but I always urge mothers to consider if the family could get along with less material goods and more mother. Would a part-time job be a better answer? Could you earn money doing something at home? There are many options for mothers who are creative and concerned about their children.

When Cornelia died, the statue erected in her memory celebrated not her wealth, rank, or title, but her motherhood. The simple inscription read, "Cornelia, the mother of the Gracchi." Cornelia, a Roman aristocrat, was the wife of Tiberius Sempronius Gracchus. Most of her children died young, but two, Tiberius and Gaius, grew up to become the famous reformers of ancient Rome's agrarian laws.

When the two Gracchi were still boys, Cornelia once received at her house a wealthy Roman lady who proudly showed off her jewelry to her hostess. She then challenged Cornelia to show off her own treasures. Cornelia gestured toward her sons, who had just entered the room. "These are my jewels," she said simply.[1]

"Mother is the name for God in the lips and hearts of children," wrote Thackeray in *Vanity Fair*. In the words of the Broadway tune, today "it ain't necessarily so." Guess what was the most popular video rented on Mother's Day in 1988? *Throw Mama From the Train*—how typical!

Where is the reverence once accorded women like Cornelia? Do you feel that your children would rather throw you from a train than erect a statue in your honor? You may struggle with motherhood. Your kids ignore you when you ask them to help with household chores and they treat your home like a barn! What's a mother to do? Where *does* a mother go to resign?

Along with motherhood are the responsibilities of being a wife. What does your husband think when he looks at you? Does he think, *Well, she's a great gal and all, but she's gained those twenty pounds since we got married, and she's not nearly as attractive as she used to be. She's disorganized, moody, and can only cook frozen foods, but hey, we're no more unhappy than anyone else.*

Has the spark gone out of your relationship? Are you lonely? Have your female friends drifted out of your life? Does your husband seem too preoccupied to notice you? Have you found yourself complaining or reminding him to do little things only to have him respond in anger? Does he accuse you of nagging? If so, the foundation of your marriage is in danger of crumbling! Before you consider having an affair or leaving your husband or before he does the same, consider what happens to the mother of a fractured family.

## Moms Get Hurt

When American families split apart, it is Mama who gets the heave-ho! She may have to sell her home, take a job, and find fulltime caregivers for her children. Suddenly she is not a wife and mother; she is a harried working woman, a coach, a disciplinarian, a counselor, a chauffeur, and the breadwinner. She is the only buffer between her family and the world, but now she is absent from home and exhausted most of the time.

Instead of being blessed by her children, many times the mother is used as a pawn by an ex-husband. When the kids visit his house, they are courted with toys, money, trips, eating out, and visions of a lifestyle far more exciting and relaxed than they find at "mother's house." Mama becomes the heavy, the resident grouch, and the penny pincher.

When my father left my mother, money was scarce. Mom, my brother, and I began a series of moves to smaller houses in lower income neighborhoods. Mom was so busy working she had little time to spend with us. When my brother was sent to my grandparents' house, I felt totally alone. My father was gone, my brother taken away, and my mother was never home.

Mom hurt for everyone. But as much as she wished circumstances could be different, she felt helpless to change them. She eventually became bitter, blaming Dad for everything that had gone wrong in our lives. The woman I had known as sweet and loving began threatening to send me to live with my Dad, whom she portrayed as a wicked and cruel man. Again, I was caught by the fear of rejection, but this time by my mother.

Mom thought she had found the answer for us when she married Bob. I was nine years old and I was ready for a daddy, even one who drank as Bob did. We bought a new house and even had a color television and a new car. *At last,* I thought, *I have a real family. Mom and I will be happy now.*

But he and Mom argued constantly. In our small neighborhood the neighbors knew everybody's business, and soon the neighbors were routinely calling the police to break up the fights between Mom and Bob.

The first time the police cars came with their lights flashing and sirens blaring, half the neighborhood came out of their houses to satisfy their curiosity. I was so embarrassed I was afraid to go out and face the kids at school the next day, but I figured the embarrassment was a small price to pay for having a dad again.

But Bob walked out on us too. When he told me to beg him to stay on that hot day in that dingy bar, I knelt, a little stubby-headed nine-year-old, and begged with all the sincerity and naïveté of childhood. With his drunken laughter ringing in my ears, I got up off that floor; my childhood ended.

Something in my mother died too. In the years that followed, things went from bad to worse. Mother constantly reached out for happiness, hoping that she would finally meet a man who would love her and stand by us, but her dreams never came true. I ignored all of the other men, determined not to get hurt again. In the meantime, my real father sank further and further into alcoholism. He lost his successful position in car sales and was unable to hold a steady job of any sort. He, too, was reaching for happiness.

I will never forget the pain I felt when I saw him with his arm around another woman. I suppose deep inside I had always hoped he would come home to us, and I was terrified when I saw him with other women. I cannot imagine what my mother felt. But she had given herself to men since that time, and failed marriages soon left her with little self-respect.

92

After working two jobs and coming home, Mom had little energy to discipline me or communicate with me. She loved me, I know, but she didn't know how to express her love. She couldn't control or discipline me either, and as I grew older and became involved in drugs and alcohol, she was frightened by what she thought I might be doing.

## The High Cost of Divorce

Mothers usually bear the brunt of divorce. Louise N. has faced an empty mailbox for over fifteen years while her four sons have been without enough shoes and clothes, have gone to bed many nights without dinner, and lived on her welfare payments for three years. She is waiting for a check for more than thirty thousand dollars her husband owes in child support.[2]

The laws which used to offer long-term alimony to divorced wives now offer short-term maintenance support intended to help former wives only until they can find a place in the work force. But problems arise when women who have spent years at home lack the advanced job skills necessary for today's employment opportunities. Women with small children who do not want to leave their children in day care must not only do so, but must pay for day care out of their meager earnings.[3]

Today only 15 percent of divorced women get any alimony and the typical award expires within twenty-five months. The woman, who 90 percent of the time gets custody of the children, gets an average custody payment of two hundred dollars a month for two children.[4]

Several mothers have described their plights after a family fracture:

"We learned to love chicken backs."

"My son had to quit the Little League and get a job as a delivery boy."

"At Christmas I splurged at the Salvation Army—the only 'new' clothes they got all year."

"I applied for welfare, though I never dreamed that I, a middle-class housewife, would ever be in a position like that. But we were desperate and I had to feed my kids."

"I finally called my parents and said we were coming."[5]

Until 1985 Karen Fox was a traditional homemaker, taking care of four children aged three to sixteen. She and her husband had a prosperous life in Westchester County, New York. Living in a five-bedroom house, they employed a gardener, a maid, and gave the children music lessons.

In September of that year, Michael Fox walked out on his family. He got a job in hotel management and moved to Texas. He set up house with a new girlfriend and despite an income of about $120,000 he was reluctant to support the family he had left behind. He often failed to make the mortgage payment and utility bills for the house in New York, which he had agreed to do under the terms of a temporary separation agreement.

Just before Christmas, Karen ran out of heating oil, her phone was disconnected, and her car was repossessed. "The kids had to go to bed with their coats on to keep warm," Karen told *Parade* magazine. Finally, she swallowed her pride and her family applied to her church for emergency relief. The only job she had been offered during her job-hunting expedition was a retail position in a department store which paid three dollars and fifty cents an hour. "That kind of money barely pays for baby-sitting," Karen said. "And, anyhow, I would have a hard time even getting to a job now that I don't have a car."[6]

## Times Have Changed

The new laws which struggle to divide property equally are bringing heartbreak to many women. California thought it had the ideal answer when it instituted a rule requiring a fifty-fifty split in divorce cases, but since the family home is often the family's only recognized asset, judges typically order it sold so that the property can be divided equally. The loss of the family home, usually designed, cared for, and run by mothers, disrupts lives, continuity, and stability.[7]

Lenore Weitzman, a sociologist, recognizes how mothers are affected by divorce. "If a court awards alimony to a woman who has spent 20 years as a homemaker and mother, it is saying it values her role and is rewarding these activities. But if a court says, 'You are not entitled to any alimony; you should go out and support yourself,' it suggests we do not value what she has done."[8] The underlying message to our mothers is clear: the only security in this world is one's own career. "That clearly undermines the whole notion of a marital partnership and penalizes those who care about children."[9]

"The divorce epidemic not only has devastated childhood, it has brought financial ruin to millions of women," stated a 1986 White House report on the American family. "Divorce reform was supposed to be a panacea for women trapped in bad marriages. It has trapped many of them in poverty."[10]

### Starting Over
The divorced mother not only faces financial difficulty, she is devastated psychologically. Author Brenda Hunter observes that along with the burden of work and the sometimes total responsibility for the care of her children, the separated or divorced mother also must contend with her own psychologi-

cal needs. "Emotionally unsupported and sometimes exploited by the men who move through her life, she may experience a succession of broken relationships and mental anguish," Hunter explains. While she puts her life back together, she is clearly pressured by a permissive culture to be sexually active. Books and articles regularly explain how to combine sex and parenting. A whole new jargon of "divorce etiquette" has emerged to absolve the divorced mother of any guilt and supply her with an arsenal of answers for her children's disturbing questions.[11]

Mothers face the difficult task of not only recovering and redirecting their own lives, but the lives of their children as well. It is mothers who often bear the brunt of explaining the divorce or separation to the children. "Only 15–20 percent of parents I work with are honest with their kids," says divorce expert Jim Smoke. "The rest of them tell their kids half-truths or nothing at all. Fathers simply walk out and mothers are left having to explain the situation."[12]

After the death of a marriage comes a time of mourning; both painful and happy memories and feelings must be sorted out and explained to the children. Mothers are the keepers of the keys of memory, and it is through their recollections that most children remember their fathers. Mothers either color those memories with honest facts, a rosy glow, or bitter castigation.

*Custody Conflicts*

During a divorce trial or custody hearing, mothers usually fight hard to keep their children—and win. According to the U.S. Bureau of the Census, in 1988 there were eighty-eight million households in the United States. Of those, two million homes consisted of a man and children; nearly ten million were homes of a woman and children.

Custodial mothers have their children at home most of the

time, but they are so busy working they have little time to spend with the kids they fought so hard to keep. It is the children who suffer from a lack of time with their mothers. Authors Ken Magid and Carole McKelvey write that divorce has caused an increase of 66 percent in the number of women who have primary responsibility for the welfare of their families. They state, "Working mothers—and the possibility that their children are suffering bonding breaks—are simply not being given enough attention."[13]

Also contributing to this problem is the continued disenfranchisement of fathers. Bobbi Williams writes of the changes in her childhood after her mother went to work: "She was always in a hurry and didn't have much time for me anymore. It was always a rush every morning to get to the sitter's. When we got home Mom always had to hurry to get supper and do her chores. When I tried to talk to her, she'd tell me to wait until later or tell me to go watch TV and be quiet. It seemed she didn't have time to be my Mom anymore."[14]

## Rebel Without a Cause?

My mother was busy working after my dad left us, and I'm sure she wondered what I did with my days and nights. I was rarely home, and I was probably doing worse things than she ever imagined. Outwardly I appeared to be a rebel with a raised fist, but inwardly I was empty and confused. My world revolved around my friends, for I had no family, and I stayed late on the streets to avoid going home to an empty shell of a house. There was nothing I cared about. Failing grades had earned me an expulsion from the football team, and nothing else interested me.

I thought about suicide and lived as though it were my next

goal. I drove at reckless speeds, took foolish risks, and spent hours idly wondering what it would be like to drive off the causeway into the gulf.

I took drugs, sold drugs, and was arrested for having and selling drugs. Three times I was sent to the Lee County Detention Center in Fort Myers, but each time I only spent one night. But one warm night in June 1970, I lost control of my car while hallucinating from drugs and hit a whole row of taxicabs, causing thousands of dollars worth of damage. I panicked, jumped out of the car, and ran away. When the police pursued and apprehended me for hit-and-run, possession, and being under the influence of drugs, I punched the arresting officer. I was sentenced to three months in the detention center, and I lost my license.

The guards who escorted me to the delousing shower thought they had a real gem. They teased me about my long hair, but I was still so high from drugs I wasn't sure what was being said to whom. I only know that I felt threatened; and I began fighting. The guard called several of his buddies and they held me down and shaved my head.

When Mom came to see me in the detention center, as she did several times, she tried to stand by me. She was confused and embarrassed, and she felt guilty. "If I had just been a better mother," she would say, staring into space. I tried to make things easier for her, but truthfully, we just didn't know each other anymore. We couldn't talk about anything, and each time she left I breathed a sigh of relief.

I spent my seventeenth birthday scrubbing floors in the detention center. No birthday cake, no party, no new car, no celebration. Only a kid down in the dirt on his knees, inwardly crying in despair and hopelessness. I had been there once before, the day I begged for a father and my childhood abruptly ended. I was beginning to think my life was over.

I know now that my mother really cared about me and was

many times the only stable force I had around me. But despite her concern, there was the ever present reality that we were not a real family. Something was missing and I knew it. I never felt like we were a real family after my father left. Like many children of divorce, I was left wondering what a real family is all about.

# 7

# What Is a Family?

**W**hat is a family? It is a simple concept with a complex definition today. Almost any group of people can declare themselves a family and be one. Traditionally, however, a family still consists of one marriage between two people of different sexes and the children that issue from, or are adopted by, the couple.

Why does the family matter so much? It is the cornerstone of American social, business, and spiritual life. A healthy family is the best place for nurturing young lives and producing productive human beings.

It is the family that supports American business. Businesses operate on the presupposition that people will want to hold a job in order to provide for their homes and children. But in America today, when new homes cost an average of $101,000 and the divorce rate is 50 percent, the erosion of the family threatens business and the fabric of American society.[1]

What are businessmen today complaining about? Many of their employees don't care, are illiterate, careless, drunk, or unwilling to learn. From where did these negative behaviors spring? From the family![2]

100

The government's debt is due in part to the erosion of the family. Millions of public dollars are diverted to fight poverty, but the main cause of poverty in the last fifteen years is divorce![3]

## Traditional Family Values

The traditional values—those espoused by generations past—work. These values—decency, integrity, honesty—are the substance of a stable society. They produce order, fulfillment, and happiness within people. "If people do not have their own order within them, it will be imposed externally. When people are too self-destructive and destructive of others, something will be done. And what will be done will resemble a police state."[4]

Traditional values within traditional families will insure the strength of the children, a higher quality way of life, and the nation. But today other families exist in addition to the traditional variety. One-parent families abound. According to the U.S. Census Bureau, the American family has declined to its smallest size ever. As of March 1987, the average family contained 3.19 members, down from 3.21 a year earlier. The total number of households has grown, but the proportion maintained by married couples has declined.[5]

It has often been reported that the "traditional" family is dead. "Traditional" in this case is used to indicate a family with a wage-earner husband, a stay-at-home wife, and two or more dependent children. Several experts indicate that only between six and ten percent of American families fit this definition.

But there are more "traditional" families than statistics lead us to believe. What about families with only one child? Or with a mother who is working only until she gives birth?

101

According to James Dobson, founder of Focus on the Family:

> The Family Service America statistics imply that 90 percent
> of American families are non-traditional. Nonsense!
> According to the U.S. Department of Labor, 47 percent of
> all adult women are at home full-time. Furthermore, of the
> 53 percent who are employed, nearly one-third work only
> part-time. That means that more than 64 percent of all
> American women are homemakers either full- or part-time,
> and included in the remaining 36 percent are single or
> childless women. Obviously, homemaking and child rearing
> are still primary responsibilities for the majority of
> American women.[6]

If you have a family of two parents plus children, you may
feel like one of the hump-back whales trapped in the ice on
the edge of extinction. Society has done little to refute that
view. *Newsweek,* for instance, has noticed that television
generally ignores the traditional, conventional American
family in favor of live-in arrangements and move-in situations. Says *Newsweek:*

> What the small screen is giving us instead is an explosion of
> sitcoms and dramas depicting almost every conceivable form
> of unconventional domestic arrangement. Call it the "move-
> in syndrome": Today's TV household finds itself obliged to
> open its doors to a throng of pushy outsiders, including
> grandparents, uncles, in-laws, orphans, housekeepers, and
> even extraterrestrial aliens . . . What's disturbing about
> prime time is that Mom and Dad are being shoved out of
> the picture—in spirit if not in body—as their function as
> authority figures becomes usurped by the ever-expanding
> influx of parental surrogates.[7]

This is frightening, because many social scientists think
that American families are greatly influenced by the families

they see on television. But television does not correctly mirror homes—it distorts them.

According to *Newsweek*, part of the problem lies with parents for allowing television to become the ultimate babysitter.[8] Twenty years ago the anonymous author of a national report proposed, "One reason that children are inclined to learn from television is that it is never too busy to talk to them."[9]

Why are parents forfeiting their parental roles of disciplinarians, lovers, and authority figures to television, teachers, and day-care workers? Are they too tired to parent, or do they just not care? Perhaps they don't know how to lead their families in a successful path.

C. S. Lewis once wrote, "The home must be the foundation of our national life. It is there, all said and done, that character is formed. It is there that we appear as we really are. It is there we can fling aside the wary disguises of the outer world and be ourselves."[10]

American families are disintegrating, but yours doesn't have to become part of the statistics. There really is only one reason for family failure today—*failure to follow God's plan for successful family living.* When His plan is rejected, the family fails.

## Building Strong Families

Christian family counselor, Dr. Ed Hindson says, "God's plan for a successful family begins with the total surrender of two lives to one another and then to God Himself."[11] A successful family can only be established on the basis of a spiritual commitment.

*I love my family,* you may think. *That's all I need to keep my family on the right track.* Is it? It all depends on how you employ your love. Love is an action verb, not a noun. You cannot passively assume your family is aware of your love; you need to be busy acting it out.

Nick Stinnett and John DeFrain have discovered six secrets of strong families. Take a moment and see how your family measures up.

### Strong Families Are Committed to One Another

"Crucial to any family's success is an investment of time, energy, spirit, and heart, an investment otherwise known as commitment. The family comes first. Family members are dedicated to promoting each other's welfare and happiness— and they expect the family to endure."[12]

Dr. Stephen A. Timm, a clinical psychologist, advises families to schedule time for family recreation in advance. "Get your calendar and plan activities and time together for the entire year. Make these times sacred and untouchable. There is a minimum amount of time that families must spend together to maintain harmony and well-being. That amount varies from family to family, but when a family drops below its minimum, problems appear."[13]

Are you committed enough to your family to cut out other activities when they begin to take away your time with your children? Have you established a strong family identity and do you regularly spend time with one another? I don't mean an annual vacation—I mean regular, established time together. Do you have, for example, one night a week which is sacred for family togetherness?

### Strong Families Spend Time Together

When fifteen hundred children were asked, "What do you think makes a happy family?" they didn't list money, cars, or fine homes. They replied, "Doing things together."

"Members of strong families agree," say Stinnett and De-

Frain. "They spend lots of time together—working, playing, attending religious services, and eating meals together. What you do isn't as important, they say, as doing it."[14]

Remember, love is an *action* verb. Get out there and do something—anything—with your family! Don't buy into the quality time myth, because children don't understand quality. They only know that parents love them if they enjoy spending time with them. Children spell love *T-I-M-E*.

One dad was amused when his little girl wanted to say the prayer of thanksgiving over the evening meal. "And Jesus, thank you that Daddy was able to come home for a visit," she prayed. That did it! The man called his next four appointments, cancelled them, and got back to the business of spending time with his family.

I should also add—strong couples spend time together. Whether you meet for lunch, telephone each other during the day, or jog together at six A.M., make a special time just for you and your spouse alone.

You should also allow yourself some personal time. "Whenever I start to feel stressed," one man told Dolores Curran, "I like to work in the garden. Sometimes when I'm bothered by work worries, my wife says, 'Why don't you go out and work on your roses for a while?' I really appreciate it when she says that."[15]

"Part of the difficulty in creating 'me' time lies in our Puritan heritage," says Curran, "which says we shouldn't play until our work is done. The reality, of course, is that our work is never done, and if we postpone those activities and friends who refresh and renew us, we find ourselves on a stressful treadmill with little pleasure in our lives."[16]

### Strong Families Show Appreciation to One Another

"Feeling appreciated by others is one of the most basic of human needs," say Stinnett and DeFrain. "As we scored ques-

105

tionnaires and conducted interviews, we found that the quantity of appreciation family members expressed to one another was even greater than anticipated. One mother wrote: 'Each night we go into the children's bedrooms and give each a big hug and kiss. Then we say, "You are really good kids and we love you very much." We think it's important to leave that message with them at the end of the day.' "[17]

How often do you thank your wife for keeping the house clean? How often do you thank your husband for working hard to support the family? Do you thank your kids for the little things they do?

I have seen several good ways for families to show appreciation for one another. Chuck Swindoll's family has a "red plate" which they pull down when a family member deserves special recognition. It's a treat and an honor to eat off the red plate!

Gloria Gaither and Shirley Dobson, in their delightful book *Let's Make a Memory*, suggest telling the kids that someone special is coming for dinner.[18] Set the table with the family china and the best linens and tell the kids to get ready for dinner. Serve the family's favorite meal. Surprise! The guests of honor are the children.

Dean and Grace Merrill, authors of *Together at Home*, have "family honor night" when one family member is selected for honor. He or she chooses the main course, decorates the table, and is guest of honor at a press conference when family members ask questions like, "What was your happiest moment today?" Then the father says a special prayer of thanks for the honored guest.

### Strong Families Communicate

"Psychologists know that good communication helps to create a sense of belonging, and eases frustrations as well as full-blown crises. Strong families emphasize that good communication doesn't necessarily happen; it usually takes time and practice."[19]

Communication is vital to a marriage and to a family. Listen carefully to what your mate and your kids are and are not telling you. Know when it is time to *listen* and when it is time to *talk*. If your feelings are hurt, don't clam up and become indifferent. If you want to be understood, you must express yourself clearly. If necessary, set aside one night a week for family discussions—a time when everyone can share frankly and listen attentively.

*Strong Families Have a Strong Religious Orientation*

"Research for several decades has shown a positive correlation of religion to marriage happiness and successful family living," says Paul Lewis, editor of the *Dads Only* newsletter. "While strong families may or may not frequently participate in organized religious activities, they do express commitment to a spiritual lifestyle. Their sense of God brings purpose and strength to their family and helps them be more patient, forgiving, positive, and supportive in their relationships."[20]

"Strong families," says Stinnett and DeFrain, "express their spiritual dimension in daily life. They literally practice what they preach. 'Our family,' one participant wrote, 'has certain values—honesty, responsibility, and tolerance, to name a few. But we have to practice those in everyday life. I can't talk about honesty and cheat on my income-tax return. I can't yell responsibility and turn my back on a neighbor who needs help. I'd know I was a hypocrite, and so would the kids and everyone else.'"[21]

In his excellent book, *Raising Positive Kids in a Negative World*, my friend, Zig Ziglar, stresses the importance of a spiritual heritage:

The spiritual aspect of man is the most important, but also

the most neglected. I believe a child's spiritual condition is the controlling factor behind what he will become. Out of the soul of man flow his attitudes, and his attitudes, not his aptitude, will determine his altitude in life. In the final analysis, the depth of his spirit will determine the height of his success.[22]

In her book, *Pathfinders*, Gail Sheehy reports the results of her study to determine what characterizes people who have a strong sense of satisfaction about themselves and their lives. In every group she surveyed, the most satisfied people were also likely to be the most religious.[23]

Dolores Curran interviewed members of happy families and found that they admitted to praying and meditating informally and in odd places: "in the car, on a commuter train, while walking or running, or during a boring meeting. Developing this deeper dimension of ourselves leads to a more harmonious relationship with our world and the people in it."[24]

One of the things that made a tremendous difference in our family was when we began to pray together on a regular basis. Learning to share our needs with one another brought us closer to each other and to God. We now take time to read the Bible, share our prayer requests, and to actually pray out loud together.

Have a family meeting and together decide that family time is an important priority to establish. Since the family is assembled, begin immediately by reading a short devotion or sharing an experience and having a prayer. Give them something to look forward to for the next scheduled time together.

Agree on a regular time and place (during nice weather, a place outdoors is refreshing) for your family worship. At first, every day may be too much to ask of busy and active children and teens; begin by getting together once a week for twenty to thirty minutes. Do not be discouraged at grumbles and complaints. Be firm and forge ahead. Remind them that everyone agreed that family worship is important. Assure them that it will be worth the effort everyone will have to make. The key is to make it interesting.

Young people and many adults may be overwhelmed with long readings of the Scripture and long prayers. Find interesting material that speaks to current issues and the heart as it teaches spiritual lessons. Involve everyone by giving them opportunities to share and ask questions, but be sensitive to anyone who is not ready to be an active participant. Each member of your family is at a different level in his or her spiritual growth. Everyone should feel safe and unthreatened by anything they choose to share.

The blessings found in your family time will be unnumbered. You will find that if you forget, your children or spouse will remind you. It will become a time of closeness, refueling, and a haven in this troubled world. Who knows . . . your family may even decide to reschedule and get together twice a week or even briefly each day!

### Strong Families Deal with Crises in a Positive Way

John DeFrain tells a story of his grandmother, Effie, who shortly before she died at age eighty-six, lay in bed blind from cataracts and suffering from complications of diabetes. Her middle-aged son, Orville, was telling her about the difficulties in his life. She listened patiently, then spoke. "Life," she told her child gently, "*is* troubles."[25]

Strong families are not without their problems. "But they have the ability to surmount life's inevitable challenges when they arise."[26]

Curran found that strong families were able to seek support from each other. She writes, "When a change of jobs, hormones, or behavior causes potential difficulties, these family members talk about it, share feelings, and come up with ways of soothing the transition. It becomes a family is-sue, and everyone takes responsibility for helping to resolve it."[27]

If a family time has been established, this becomes the time to support and undergird members who are in trouble and need the strength of the others. If you have not begun having a regular time together, it is never too late to start. If the father is faltering in his faith, then this is the time for the mother to step in and see that the family holds tightly to him and continues to be his oasis. It may even be the voice of a child that brings the family back together. Listen to that voice and follow its leading.

Strong families know that no progress is made up the mountain of life unless there are bumps to climb on. It is through trial and testing that people become stronger. It is through difficulty that a person pulls tightly into the fabric of his family, and in doing so, finds love, peace, and the strength to carry on.

When the pressures of life come your way, only a solid spir-itual foundation will enable you to withstand the storms of life. As your children grow up, they need to see the consistent example of a mom and dad who pray together, talk together, worship together, and who, above all else, are committed to making their marriage last.

# 8

# Tamper-Proof Marriages

The threat of an anonymous, random killer forced the makers of Tylenol and other products to design tamper-proof packaging. Today if you buy Tylenol in a drugstore, you will find a sealed box; a cellophane-covered, child-resistant cap; an inner foil seal, and "gelcaps"—capsules which are enclosed in gelatin so the seal cannot be broken. There are at least four lines of defense against contamination and each of those seals, if broken, makes it clearly evident to the consumer that something is wrong.

Wouldn't it be great if tamper-proof marriages could be designed? Actually, there are lines of defense and warning signals that something is about to go wrong in a marriage. Sociologist Diane Vaughan believes there are several warning signs that a marriage is headed for a painful breakup.

## Warning Signs

*Keeping Secrets*
"When you fall in love," says Vaughan, "you pay attention to every word, to every expression, to everything your partner

is doing. But as a relationship ages, communication reverts to shorthand. When feelings of unhappiness creep into the picture, they may remain largely unspoken because of ambivalence or fear. Instead the person who is dissatisfied—the initiator—begins to display discontent through cues and hints, such as a disgruntled glance, a goodnight kiss omitted, an activity that conflicts with a time understood to be 'our time.'"[1]

## Communication Fails

"It's a good thing Mary loves Tom," said Sue to her husband as they left Mary and Tom's home. "Because she certainly picks at him a lot. I've never seen two couples argue the way they do, but I guess that is just their way."

Constant picking and criticism is *not* the way of happily married couples, as Sue learned. Within six months Mary had left Tom for good. When communication begins to fail, so does a marriage.

If the unhappy spouse turns to the other and clears the air through good communication, the problems can be resolved. But if he or she turns to someone else, a confidante outside the marriage, another warning signal rears its head.

## Trading Roles

Your spouse should be your lover, your romantic interest, and your best friend. If any of those roles are assigned to another person, the marriage is on stormy ground.

If the wayward spouse finds a new best friend and that friend becomes a romantic interest or even a lover, the marriage relationship is doomed. "The initiator has found a separate social niche," says Vaughan, "and the burden of saving the relationship falls on the partner. While the initiator is busy enumerating the negative qualities of the relationship, the partner will try to focus on the positive."[2]

112

## *Clutching at Straws*

Many men and women fall into this trap. They know their marriage is in trouble, so they throw pride to the wind in order to save their marriage. They try to lose weight, improve their minds, keep a cleaner house, or remake themselves into what they think their spouse wants and needs.

"As a love affair begins to deteriorate," writes James Dobson. "The vulnerable partner is inclined to panic. Characteristic responses include grieving, lashing out, begging, pleading, grabbing and holding; or the reaction may be just the opposite, involving appeasement and passivity.

"While these reactions are natural and understandable, they are rarely successful in repairing the damage that has occurred. In fact, such reactions are usually counterproductive, destroying the relationship the threatened person is trying so desperately to preserve."[3]

If you find yourself in this position, you owe it to yourself and your marriage to read James Dobson's *Love Must be Tough*. Dr. Dobson's advice is sound—based on experience and Scripture.

## An Ounce of Prevention

If your marriage is not at the breaking point, how can you make certain it will never be?

Have you chosen to love your mate? Some people marry with a pricetag on their love. They say, "I will love you *if* . . .

> . . . you surrender;
> . . . you make me happy;
> . . . you stay gorgeous;
> . . . you pay the bills and provide for me."

Others marry and say, "I love you because . . .

**113**

. . . you make me feel good;
. . . you're cute;
. . . we're a good team;
. . . you need me.

These things are important, but they should not be the basis of love. If you love someone because of a certain quality, what happens to your love when that quality changes?

A man and woman should stand before each other and choose to say, "I love you." Complete, giving, unconditional love should be offered. This is the love God shows to man. This is the love husbands and wives should share. This kind of love cements a man and woman together for a lifetime.

When you stood before a minister or public official and took your marriage vows, you promised to "love, honor, and cherish 'till death do us part." You left the home of your mother and father behind in order to form a new family with the man or woman who stood by your side.

Your marriage vows were an oath made between you, your spouse, and God Himself. In *The Mystery of Marriage,* Mike Mason writes:

> The meaning of the marriage vows finds its deepest
> resonance, then, in the biblical concept of covenant, in
> which two parties so bind themselves to one another that
> the simple maintenance of their relationship becomes the
> most important and central thing in all of life, the basis
> from which everything else flows.[4]

A covenant is a life and death agreement which expresses the ultimate commitment which can be made between two people or between God and a person. Your marriage covenant, which lasts for a lifetime, is the most important vow you will make in life aside from the commitment you may choose to make to Jesus Christ as Lord and Savior.

In Genesis 2:24 God explains the mystery of marriage:

"Therefore a man shall leave his father and mother and be joined to his wife, and they shall become one flesh." Husbands and wives should consider each other as an extension of themselves. This thought is also echoed and explained in Ephesians 5:28: "So husbands ought to love their own wives as their own bodies; he who loves his wife loves himself."

When God brought Eve to Adam, Adam recognized that she was literally an extension of himself. She was not made from the clay as he had been, but had been created from his bone, his flesh. Adam and Eve were dependent upon each other; both were dependent upon the Lord.

In order to find this sense of "one flesh," marriage partners must know each other. Part of knowing each other is understanding the little quirks and the habits that annoy you, yet accepting them.

Knowing each other means being able to apologize and receive forgiveness, not hold a grudge. Holding a grudge might provide you with some self-pity or make the other person feel bad, but it will accomplish little else.

How important is your marriage to you? Are you willing to give a little to gain a lot? No one is suggesting you be a doormat, only that you be willing to forgive in the same manner that you want to be forgiven. Everyone is capable of doing and saying some pretty nasty things. But forgiveness binds you together and keeps you growing in one direction.

Knowing each other does *not* mean finishing sentences, anticipating reactions, and making decisions based on previous negative situations. Marriage partners must allow room for change, growth, and new patterns.

## Learning to Love

Years ago I prayed, "Lord, please send me a girl whom I can love and who will love me. Lord, send me someone who

will love You and help me be strong in my faith. I need someone to love who will help me not to fall."

God gave me that person, Diane, and I was thrilled. But
soon after we were married some problems developed. I
didn't understand this. We loved each other very much, but
the arguments kept coming. I made up my mind that I would
not allow *my* marriage to end like the ones of my childhood.
Something had to be done.

I graduated cum laude with a Bachelor of Arts degree in
two and a-half years. It was hard work, but not hardly as
difficult as becoming a good husband. I began reading every
book about marriage I could get my hands on, and I began to
pray, "Lord, change *me*" instead of "Lord, change *her!*"
Diane prayed in the same way.

What I discovered was that I had never learned how to love
or express my feelings. I had grown up unwilling to trust anyone because those closest to me had hurt me emotionally. I
had never spoken the words "I love you" to anyone until I was
eighteen years old. All of this had to be dealt with before I
could grow in my marriage.

My wife grew up surrounded by love and trust. She expected the same of me and was discouraged when I could not
give it. Together we made the decision to help each other. She
was patient with me and I tried to understand her needs.

It did not happen overnight, but through the course of
opening our feelings to one another, we began to trust and
believe in one another. Diane had to realize that certain
things she said or did would always bring an angry reaction
in me. While I recognized that this anger was wrong, I still
needed her to help me by not dangling it in front of me. She
helped me realize that she needed to know she was important
to me and that I respected her. Many times I did not treat her
unkindly, I simply ignored her. It was not because I did not
love her; I simply did not know how to show that love.

A deficiency of communication like ours can come from many sources: a lack of interest in the marriage (usually because of competing interest in a career or self), an inability to communicate, insecurity, the fear of facing problems, and ignorance.

Diane and I concentrate on communicating to one another. She has told me that she tries to think *how* to present her needs or problems rather than blurt them out in a way that will confuse both of us. We are both concentrating on responding rather than reacting to each other's words.

We often recognize problems or bad habits in each other. We would have a constant civil war if we made snide or accusing remarks about these problems, but we try to gently help the other see the problems. Light-hearted wit can work wonders.

Taking the time to work on the problems in your relationship does not signal serious trouble or unhappiness. It is your greatest source of prevention. If more couples would attend marriage seminars *before* problems occur, there would probably be fewer divorces. Marriage is meant to be enjoyed, and too many people are just enduring what could bring them incredible delight.

To circumvent problems, couples should establish priorities and moral values together so that the lines are clearly drawn. When one strays or begins to stray from the established guidelines, discussion must take place immediately. Husbands and wives need each other's help in their spiritual and moral lives. They are one flesh, and as two arms balance the body, so they must continually balance each other in love.

Unconditional love means being accepted just the way you are, just for the life you have already shared, without expecting your needs to be met but rather sacrificing yourself to meet the needs of your spouse. I once heard James Dobson say that he came to the place where he realized that if his wife never did another thing to please him, he would have reason enough to love her the rest of his life because of the times they had shared together.

Love simply for the sake of loving. Until you love unconditionally you do not have true love. When love is freely given, it will automatically be reciprocated. If you make your partner feel good, he or she will return the favor. You reap what you sow in a marriage relationship.

If you are looking for what you can get out of marriage, your marriage will never work. Only as you give will you be given to. Just because you woke up today with your selfish heart saying, "I'm ready to quit; I don't want to try anymore," does not mean it is time to throw in the towel. Quitting only leaves you lonely and with many more problems.

Love is more than saying "I love you." It is showing that you care. Ask "How are you feeling? How is work? What can I do to help you today?" Pledge to share your deepest hurts and greatest joys. Ask each morning, "How can I pray for you today?"

Love as though there is no tomorrow. If today was the very last day you had to live, how would you live it? Would you be concerned about petty details, or would you make the day an occasion for love?

Learn to distinguish between what is major and minor. Learn to forgive and be understanding about the little annoyances that rock the boat of marital bliss.

When arguments do arise, determine the root cause quickly. Many times couples fight because of their negative thinking. They allow themselves to dwell on "the last time" and the past, and soon what began as an insignificant quibble becomes an insurmountable obstacle. If you think in the back of your mind that your marriage will not work, it *never will*. Positive attitudes and a willingness to work it out are essential to a successful marriage.

Take the time to write down the good qualities of your spouse and memorize them. Think on them throughout the day. Thank him or her for those attributes often. Before long you will notice that the list is growing.

Have fun together! If I have a day off to spend with anyone I choose, I will always choose my wife. She is my best friend and we enjoy each other's company. We have fun and lift each other up.

There is nothing we would rather do than hire a babysitter and take off into town for a date. We tend to forget about the petty problems, like the leaky faucet, and we learn again how to concentrate on each other.

I constantly hear couples sigh, "We have nothing in common. I simply cannot communicate with that man." The word *communicate* means literally "to have in common." It is obvious that so many couples no longer communicate because they have not taken the time to develop common interests. They do not have fellowship together—you know, like two fellows in the same ship!

If you are serious about building fellowship, dig out your old stationery and try your hand at penning those sweet love notes you used to send while you were courting. My wife writes me cards and letters of encouragement. She thanks me for things I have done for her, some big and some small, but when she takes the time to comment on them, I know they were special to her. She points out positive attributes that I cannot see, and all of this causes me to love her so much more.

I write her love notes too. I tell her how much I love her and why I love her. She tells me these touch her in a way that nothing else can.

Your love notes do not have to be mushy. They do not have to be long. Just take the time to jot down a few words of encouragement or positive affirmation. You will be amazed at the results.

## The Joy of Intimacy

Your marriage relationship is intended to be one of great fulfillment and joy. Dr. John Cuber has found that many couples remain married simply for the sake of their children. Others pass the years in relative apathy. Only one or two couples out of ten will achieve true intimacy in marriage.[5] By intimacy, I refer to the mystical bond of friendship, commitment, and understanding that exists between a husband and wife. It is the same mystical union which joins Christ to His church.

This intimacy, which involves the mind, emotions, and body, includes sexual intimacy. Sexual intercourse is the physical expression of becoming "one flesh." In their book, *The Act of Marriage*, Tim and Beverly LaHaye discuss the physical marriage union:

> Evidence of God's blessings on this sacred relationship
> appears in the charming expression used to describe the act
> of marriage between Adam and Eve in Genesis 4:1: "and
> Adam knew Eve his wife; and she conceived . . ." What
> better way is there to describe the sublime, intimate
> interlocking of mind, heart, emotions, and body in a
> passionately eruptive climax that engulfs the participants in
> a wave of innocent relaxation that thoroughly expresses their
> love? The experience is a mutual "knowledge" of each other
> that is sacred, personal, and intimate. Such encounters were
> designed by God for mutual blessing and enjoyment.[6]

Unfortunately, today's movies and music make sex little more than a physical act, as casually enjoyed with semi-strangers as with your spouse. But sex was designed to be an act of total intimacy between two people who know and are committed to one another. If you doubt this, read the Song of Solomon with new eyes. This book of the Bible is a song of praise for married love—emotional, spiritual, and physical.

Mike Mason beautifully describes sex between a husband and wife:

> We may not think of the removal of clothes as being a revelation of our thoughts and character, but that in fact is exactly what happens . . . For they have become one flesh as surely as if their very nervous systems had been coupled together into the same computer network. Thereafter, what one knows, the other knows also with the deep and secret knowledge of the flesh, and they needn't kid themselves that this is not the case.[7]

Does this describe your marriage? Are you and your spouse truly "one flesh"? Most family counselors agree with medical studies that less than one percent of the world's population have any physical reason for sexual incompatibility. The real barrier is psychological.

## Barriers to Intimacy

There are several emotional blocks that develop in marriage which contribute to the lack of intimacy and spontaneity. Financial uncertainty, family quarrels, and other stress-producing conditions are among the blocks of sexual expression in marriage. Proper sexual expression between a couple is not an act but an outgrowth of genuine love which includes trust, admiration, respect, and affection. A couple must get along in the living room, the family room, and the work room if they expect to get along in the bedroom.

Esteem is the basis for intimacy. "I love you" must never be interpreted, "I love me and want to use you." We sing about love, write poetry about love, and talk about love, but the word has lost its original and true meaning.

The ancient Greeks used three different words to define and communicate the three dimensions of what we try to project in one word. A lasting and fulfilling marriage needs all three aspects of love: *eros, philia,* and *agape.*

*Eros. Eros* is the word which conveys romantic and sexual love. It is the love that seeks sensual expression. In a fulfilling marriage, the husband and wife will express their love in a romantic, sensual way.

Sexuality is part of your human nature given to you by the Creator. The Bible teaches that sex is a gift of God meant to be enjoyed by His creation. The book of Genesis teaches us that sex fulfills a *specific task*—Adam and Eve were instructed to be fruitful and multiply.

Man and woman were created to meet each other's needs. God clearly stated, "It is not good for man to be alone." He further said, "The two shall become one flesh." The sexual act is also a *sacred trust*. The intimacy shared by two people is incomparable to any other act or interaction. The intimacy is then developed into a trust and sharing of emotions and a security of being able to disclose even the deepest and most personal feelings. True love moves sexual intercourse beyond pleasure into a bonding experience. A realization of this intimacy rules out adultery and fornication.

Sexual intimacy is also a *satisfying treat*. To view sex as only a physical satisfaction is to miss out on the total benefits of the marriage relationship. Yes, sexual intercourse is the greatest thrill known to mankind. No wonder society is infactuated with sex.

The *Criswell Study Bible* notes six distinct purposes of sexual intimacy: knowledge (Gen. 4:1), unity (Gen. 2:24), comfort (Gen. 24:67), procreation (Gen. 1:28), relaxation and play (Song of Sol. 2:8–17; 4:1–16), and avoidance of temptation (1 Cor. 7:5).[8]

Never use sex as a punishment or display of anger. You only push your spouse into temptation. Extramarital sex is available on every corner, in the workplace, and even in the church.

*Philia.* *Philia* is the love that is based on common interests and goals. Our word *like* comes closest to this meaning. As one recently engaged couple said, "I know we'll be happy because we're buddies. We've been friends for a long time."

*Philia* refers to human affection and concern, two requirements for every successful growing marriage. Mates are not only lovers but friends as well. One recently divorced couple told me, "We still love each other—we just don't like each other." This couple did not have friendship at the core of their relationship because the development of their love was not based on mutual interests. You must enjoy each other's company.

*Agape.* *Agape* is self-giving, sacrificial love. This is the word used all through Scripture to describe God's love for you. It is loving without regard to merit; it is unconditional love. It is loving when the object of that love is sometimes unloveable. This love is measured by sacrifice, by a willingness to give.

There will be times when *eros* is running on empty and *philia* is faint. Then *agape* bridges the gap and is the sustaining power of the relationship. That is why it is important to develop spiritually as well as emotionally.

The thirteenth chapter of First Corinthians details the attributes of a godly, unconditional love. Each couple should read this individually and then together. Study it, memorize it, and refer to it often. Man's love can and does "run out," but God's love will always be there to pick up the slack and fuel the other dimensions of love.

Tim Timmons, who holds national marriage enrichment seminars, explains that "oneness" in marriage is achieved by receiving, not merely accepting, your mate as a special gift from God to complete you where you are incomplete. A maximum marriage happens when the man and the woman come into dynamic and intimate oneness and through that oneness find themselves individually. Timmons uses humor to describe the typical growth of a marriage: "There are three phases: the ideal, the ordeal, and the new deal."[9]

## Steps to Success

You can pass from the *ordeal* to the *new deal* and have a "tamper-proof" marriage if you follow the suggestions listed below:

*Discuss your marriage vows with your mate.* Agree with each other that you will choose to love each other until death parts the two of you.

*Make the effort to make sure your spouse remains your best friend, your romantic interest, and your lover.* Allow no one else to usurp any of those roles. Instead, work hard to improve your relationship with your spouse.

*Keep communication open.* Do not go to bed if there is something bothering you or your spouse. Discuss it and work through it. Use respectful communication and words like *please* and *thank-you.* Recognize that each of you has different needs and respect those needs. Give each other individual space and time alone, then schedule time to be together. Make your times together fun, not simply work "in the line of duty."

*Find the good things about your husband or wife and celebrate them.* Give your spouse at least one sincere compliment each day.

*Learn to forgive and do not bring up the failures of the past.* Real forgiveness involves total forgetfulness in how you treat each other's past mistakes.

*Do not let small problems grow into big ones.* Resolve them early by dealing with them as soon as possible.

*Set aside regular time for "just the two of you" to go on a date or a weekend retreat.* Even though you are married, continue giving the attention, courtesy, and courtship which accompanied your dating.

*Let your children know that you love each other.* Be affectionate around your home. You are modeling marriage for them, and they will base their idea of the ideal mate upon your example. Your child will either say, "I want to marry someone just like you" or "I'll find someone who is the complete opposite."

There are no easy solutions to life's difficulties. But there are basic principles which can make a difference in your life. Once you are willing to commit yourself to make your marriage work, God can bless you beyond your greatest expectations. He alone can break down the barriers and bring true and lasting healing into your life and marriage.

# 9

# When Walls Go Up
# Between Us

Even though it happened years ago, I can still close my
eyes and hear my parents arguing. My father, angry and
drunk, once yelled at my mother, "I can't think of a single
reason to stay married to you."

From my hiding place in my room, I thought, *I'll be that
reason. Surely he'll stay here if he loves me.* I tried so hard to
be a good kid, but when Dad finally walked out that door
and did not return, I was devastated. To my father, I wasn't a
good enough reason for staying at home. *If I was worth anything*, I thought, *he would have stayed*.

A school teacher I know once asked her high school class if
they ever lay in bed and listen to their parents arguing. In
unison, the class nodded, their eyes quiet and sober. Even in
stable marriages, fighting makes kids of all ages feel frightened and insecure. Parents may wait until after the kids have
gone to sleep to bring up an unpleasant discussion, but children invariably wake up when stressful voices fill the house.

As a kid sometimes the silence in my house was even more
disturbing. It was normal for my folks to bicker with each
other, but when they fell silent I knew something was definitely wrong. They were like strangers living and moving

around in the same house. They played a silent game with each other, and I was confused and left out. I didn't know the rules, but I knew that no one would come out of that game a winner.

## "Talk to Me"

Half of all the brides choosing a wedding dress today will be divorced in five years.[1] One of the major reasons for this will be a lack of communication. Research shows that the average career couple only talks to each other thirteen minutes a day![2] We live in such a fast-paced society that we now have drive-through diners and even drive-through zoos! People are working more and making more money but enjoying life less than ever.

Too many people think that communication is automatic. *We're in love, we're married, and we're happy,* the young couple may think. *We'll never have a problem communicating.* But after a few months of marriage, they meet at home for dinner. He pecks her cheek and settles back into his easy chair while she begins preparing dinner.

HE: *(reading the paper)* Did you have a good day at work?
SHE: No, I had a lousy day today. I woke up with a headache and my boss didn't tell me about the board meeting which I was supposed to prepare for. When I forgot, he yelled at me.
HE: *(still reading)* H-m-m . . . that's nice.
SHE: You're not listening.
HE: Sure I am. You have a headache.
SHE: You didn't hear a word I said.
HE: I heard the important part. I don't want to hear about your troubles right now, I'm trying to relax. I had a hard day at work too.

Genuine communication is hard work and it is not easy. It is a risky venture undertaken by two people who are willing to be totally honest and intimate with each other. Communication is honest without being critical.

I was surprised when Bob called me in the middle of the day. I had just spent several days with him and his lovely wife, a talented young woman who was the backbone of their church. "Jay, I need help in my marriage," Bob blurted out.

As his story unfolded, I became aware that the priorities in their marriage were confused. Bob wanted so much to enjoy a fulfilling marriage, but his wife placed her energy into the church. She was attractive, moral, good, and well-liked by everyone. What more could a man want? Just a little love and attention. Bob needed a chance to show his love and care. He wanted to be a partner, not a bystander.

Because Bob's wife was so fulfilled and happy in what she was doing, she could not understand what the problem was. He needed her emotionally, physically, and spiritually. She simply wasn't putting as much work and emotion into their relationship as she did into her public work. Bob had to sit her down and honestly share his feelings.

Joe and Cathy are always late. Joe silently blames Cathy; he has never said anything about his anger. Tonight they are going to a party at his boss' house, and Cathy, as usual, is running behind schedule.

"Honey," Joe calls. "We need to leave in five minutes."

"I can't, dear," Cathy calls from the bathroom. "I don't have my makeup on yet."

Joe stews for a moment, then rushes into the bathroom, his suppressed anger exploding. "I'm sick and tired of always being late," he yells. "We're a joke. Everyone knows that we are always late."

"Well, honey," Cathy tries to calm him down, "the problem is just that you don't give me enough time to get ready."

"You've got all day!" yells Joe. "The real problem is just that you're lazy. I hate being late!"

A misunderstanding has grown into personal confrontation and attack. Not only is Joe angry about being late, but now he has attacked his wife and sunk to the level of name-calling.

I counseled another couple and had to agree with the husband—his wife did make a lot of mistakes. Her husband patiently pointed each one out and gave her a lecture on mending her ways, but somehow she seemed to make the same mistake the next day.

Her husband was embarrassed and had lost all respect for the woman he married. He resigned himself to telling her she was "crazy," and decided he had married a dummy with no sense at all.

I couldn't help noticing the woman's face. Her eyes showed her fright and insecurity, and it never occurred to her to question why her husband did not love her. *Surely,* she thought, *I am as worthless as he says I am!*

But this couple needed to learn to see each other—and themselves—with new eyes. By magnifying her errors, he never noticed the things she did do well. His own need for perfection, fueled by his own insecurities, was destroying the self-esteem of his wife.

They learned to reorganize. She learned to set goals for work and home and accomplish them a step at a time. He learned to look for her good qualities and found that as he admired and praised her, she became a more positive person.

## When Tough Times Come

It is not only trivial problems which block communication. Serious problems often cause a breakdown in communication. David and Trudy Burke of Johnstown, Pennsylvania were interviewed by *Newsweek* magazine. David lost his job and soon the Burke family showed signs of trouble. David and Trudy tried to cheer each other up, but soon their communication disintegrated as David became more and more depressed. He simply would not talk, or if he tried, they simply did not communicate on the same level.

Eventually they began seeing a therapist in order to save their home and marriage. Gradually they found each other again and learned to talk through their hurts and disappointments. Says David: "You can't have a monologue."[3] Communication is essential.

## Learning to Listen

Communication is more than words. A few years ago Kodak did a study to determine exactly what influences communication. The researchers discovered that the actual spoken words account for only 7 percent of the total message! Thirty-eight percent of the message is conveyed in the tone of voice used; and a staggering 55 percent of the message is communicated through body language—eye contact, facial expression, hand gestures, and how close the speaker is to the one he is addressing.

When you talk to your spouse, do you rattle on with your mouth while your hands are busy preparing dinner? Or do you simply mumble from behind the pages of the newspaper? How long has it been since you sat down with your spouse and talked about your goals, dreams, ideas, and childhood?

I travel extensively in my work and there are many nights when I am away from my wife and children. So when I am home, I know it is important to spend time with my family. I enjoy listening to the kids talk and playing games with them.

It is also important to discuss the children and all of the other things which have filled my wife's day.

But there are other times when I need to be alone with just my wife. We discuss the ministry and I ask her opinion about many things. Her communication is a valuable gift to me. I have been married for sixteen years and there are still things I don't know about that woman! I know her better than I know any human being on this earth, but she is a jewel with new facets to be discovered and enjoyed.

We have found that our differences can be worked out through everyday experiences. She teaches a women's Sunday school class, and because I also enjoy teaching the Bible, I often try to help her out with ideas. In fact, I used to call her from out of town and discuss her lessons with her.

Of course, I always thought this was pure kindness on my part, but one day my wife looked at me and asked, "Honey, do you think I am unable to study and come up with some ideas of my own?" She went on to explain that she felt smothered by my help, and she needed some space to be creative and try out her own ideas. She needed me to show confidence in *her* abilities.

Not one to let an opportunity slip by, I told her that I understood exactly how she felt, for I often felt the same way when she made suggestions about the running of my office. We ended the conversation in a tie—we had both scored a point!

What robs couples of communication? I believe the primary thief today is the television set! In too many families, communication is limited to television's commercial breaks. Consider the following which first appeared in a letter to Ann Landers:

> In the house
> Of Mr. and Mrs. Spouse

He and she
Would watch TV,
And never a word
Between them was spoken
Until the day
The set was broken.
Then, "How do you do?"
Said He to She.
"I don't believe we've met.
"Spouse is my name.
"What's yours?" he asked
"Why, mine's the same!"
Said She to He.
"Do you suppose we could be . . . ?"
But the set came suddenly right about
And they never did find out.[4]

Jim Powers, a marriage and family counselor for employees of the A. L. Williams Insurance Company, offers three keys to good communication:

1. *We should be able to share our hearts without fear of rebuke, ridicule, or correction.* Allow your spouse to express his or her opinions and feelings openly and honestly.

2. *We should have an unconditional love and acceptance of our mate.* Without total commitment your relationship will never become all that it could be.

3. *We should practice the art of listening.* Good listening requires energy. Good listening requires resisting the urge to jump into the conversation prematurely with your own ideas and opinions. Good listening requires as much physical effort as speaking.[5]

Jim's wife, Maripat, was busy in the kitchen one afternoon when their son Joshua returned home from school. He was babbling about someone at school, then he suddenly stopped and questioned, "Mommy, are you listening?"

"Yes, honey, I'm listening," Maripat replied.

"No, Mommy. Listen to me with your face!"

Maripat put down her work and stooped down to Josh's level. "OK, sweetheart," she answered. "Now I'm listening with *all* of me."

Careful listening is vital to good communication. Allow your spouse to express his or her feelings without interruption or correction. If you do not understand exactly what was being expressed, ask gently for further explanation. At all costs, avoid criticism and sweeping generalizations that condemn the person you are married to: "That's crazy! You're absolutely nuts if you think like that!" No one wants to open up his heart if his ideas are going to be trampled underfoot.

Dr. Michael Zwell says attention is the most important part of communication. "Listening well means paying attention to other people and not shifting the attention onto ourselves or away from them in any other way. Looking at them, not thinking about something else while they are talking—these are all attributes of attentive behavior."[6]

## Opening Up and Letting It Out

It is not easy to communicate with another person. On the whole, boys and girls grow up and are encouraged to communicate on different levels. Girls are encouraged to share their feelings and have friends with whom they talk and tell their secrets. Boys interact with each other through the physical activities of play and sports. In this country boys are not encouraged to show emotion—"big boys don't cry."

When these same girls and boys grow up and marry, they are still relating on different levels. The girls try to talk and share, and not only do the guys not know how to do this, they usually do not know how to listen and respond. They are still communicating through work and play. Men are not used to sharing deep feelings—many cannot even identify and verbalize them at all. Wives want to be with their husbands and talk to them; they want to be heard and understood. Most husbands want to communicate with their wives on a deeper level and are willing to learn.

One of the greatest gifts you can give your children is teaching them how to communicate and share their feelings. Again, the best way to teach and encourage open communication is to be a good model.

*Communication* literally means to "have in common" or "to share equally." How can you share with each other when men and women approach life from different perspectives?

First, learn to share life with each other. Find a quiet time when you can share not only your experiences (what happened during the day, etc.) but also your ideas and your dreams. *Know* each other. What makes your mate angry? What makes him happy? *Think* before you speak. You will some day give an account to God for every idle word you have spoken, so think carefully before you open your mouth.

Second, meet each other's needs. Men and women have different needs and you cannot meet your mate's needs unless you understand what those are.

Ed and Carol Neuenschwander have been married for over twenty years. They believe marriage is renewed through romance, and romance is the natural result of "really focusing on each other's lives." The Neuenschwanders offer advice about how to urge a quiet spouse to open up:

> If the husband or wife is uncommunicative, literally
> celebrate the times when he or she does communicate. A
> wife could say, "I'm so glad you told me that. You don't
> realize how great I feel when I know what you're thinking
> and feeling." Be positive. Women tend to nag and say, "I

wish you would . . ." when they should be saying, "I'm so glad you do . . . ," A woman who knows how to show love and appreciation will go far in keeping the doors of communication open.[7]

Are you building walls that prohibit communication? If you decide to begin again and tear those walls down, just do not start throwing the bricks at each other!

## Attack the Problem, Not Each Other

Did you know all arguing is not bad? I know a couple who divorced after thirty years of marriage. Both said, "To everyone else we looked perfect, but we have had no relationship for years." They didn't have anything, not even a good argument!

To argue is better than not to discuss at all. Don't be afraid of an argument, but do have ground rules before you start. Keep in mind these ideas for "constructive arguing":

*Fight fair*. Keep the issues current. Don't dig up old arguments and rehash them. One woman said, "I buried the hatchet, but I know just where to dig it up!" Remember, the intention of your discussion is to come to an agreement, not to get *your* way.

*Keep it light*. When things start to get out of hand, stop to reevaluate. How important is it that you get your point across? What is more important—the issue or your pride?

If the discussion has no direction, you may find yourself coming out with ridiculous statements. My wife and I have a standard. Once I made a declaration so absurd that we stopped arguing and broke out into hysterical laughter! We remember that line and use it on each other if an argument begins to get out of hand.

*Evaluate the source of the problem.* Ask each other when this started, how it started, and why it started. Be willing to work hard to get at the root rather than just yowling about the symptoms.

*Listen.* The object of the discussion is concerned with two viewpoints, yours and your mate's. By listening you show that you care, you are interested, and that your spouse is important to you. You also show that you are open to admitting where you are wrong.

*Offer solutions.* The goal is to cure the problem, not to spend endless hours in argument. You want to understand, not be declared the "winner."

*Consider the environment.* Where and how you are feeling at the time of the discussion may have a profound effect on how you communicate. If you know your spouse, you can be aware of the best as well as the most unproductive times for a discussion.

*Continue until restoration occurs.* It would be easier to quit in the middle or to avoid arguing altogether, but this will hurt rather than help. "Never go to bed angry" is good advice. It comes from the Bible where God says, "Don't let the sun go down on your wrath." Hurt must be resolved and forgiveness must be settled even if the solution is not yet apparent.

*Don't yell.* Yelling signals a loss of control and the discussion cannot go any further. Yelling usually happens when the problem has been allowed to "stew" too long or if other outside problems are aggravating the situation. If someone starts to yell, back up and start over or wait until you can speak in a civil manner.

*Timing can make the difference. I have a right to be angry, and I'm going to be angry!* you may think, but though your anger may not be wrong, your timing may be. Are you going to take a small problem and launch it into a major disaster when time alone would cause it to assume its true insignificance? Consider *when* and *how* you are going to argue, and don't let the heat of the moment carry you into a violent fray.

If you are still angry about an issue after the heat of the moment has passed, make your stand. Psychologist Les Carter states in his book *Push-Pull Marriage*, "Anger is nothing more than making an emotional stand for one's convictions."[8] See it as healing balm rather than as burning acid.

## Spread Some Praise

Henry Ferguson writes that he and his wife once stopped by a New England apple cider stand where an elderly farmer and his wife greeted him. As they sipped cider, the old farmer remarked that he and his wife had been happily married for nearly fifty years. He added, "I reckon the best marriages are really mutual-admiration societies. Elsie likes a little compliment from time to time—and so do I."[9]

A biblical proverb reminds us to the importance of affirmation and praise: "Pleasant words are like a honeycomb, sweetness to the soul and health to the bones" (Prov. 16:24). Have you given your spouse a regular dose of pleasant words?

Or are you more pleasant and polite to the mail carrier than you are to your spouse?

Dennis and Barbara Rainey say that words are like seeds. "Once planted in your mate's life, your words will bring forth flowers or weeds, health or disease, healing or poison. You carry a great responsibility for their use. As Proverbs 18:21 says, 'Death and life are in the power of the tongue.' Your words have the power to contaminate a positive self-image or to heal the spreading malignancy of a negative one."[10]

Mark Twain once said that he could "live for two months on a good compliment." Try giving a genuine, sincere compliment to your spouse and see how long the glow lasts.

Everyone needs admiration and appreciation. They need respect. Too often words of honesty come out sounding like criticism. A person cannot feel the respect of a spouse if that spouse is constantly being belittled, especially in public.

It is easy to get into the habit of criticism. Ed and Carol Neuenschwander write, "Criticism can become an unquenchable appetite, a way of life, and there can be just as vicious a battle to overcome it as to overcome greed, lust, anger, or controlled substances and chemicals. It's best to stop it in its earlier stages. Criticism kills."[11]

Sarcasm is nothing but criticism with a humorous edge. Trouble is, the humor is usually only in the mind of the speaker—not the listener.

"Honey, you don't really need to order dessert, do you?" asks a man when he and his wife are out to dinner with friends. "After all, didn't you break the bathroom scales this week?"

Ha ha. He thinks he is being funny; his wife thinks he couldn't possibly love her anymore. What man destroys a woman he loves?

Everyone needs to be shown respect, honest admiration, attention, and affection. Your spouse needs to be number one on your "love list." Each person wants to feel secure in the love of his or her partner and in the permanence of the home. A person needs to feel attractive and appreciated in the eyes of his or her mate. Each person is an individual with separate needs. It is the responsibility of the partner to discover and to help fulfill those needs whenever possible.

In his classic work *How to Win Friends and Influence People*, Dale Carnegie tells the story of Disraeli, a man who once stated that he never intended to marry for love. Disraeli did not marry until he was thirty-five; but then he proposed to a rich widow several years his senior.

Disraeli and his wife, Mary Anne, found a richness in marriage which surpasses what most people know today. Mary Anne knew Disraeli married her for money and friendship, not love, so they became the best of friends. She was somewhat dizzy, always babbling in society about trivial affairs, but Disraeli honored her because she never criticized him, never bored him, and always respected him.

They were married for thirty years and a happier home could not be found. Disraeli persuaded Queen Victoria to elevate Mary Anne to the peerage; in 1868 she was made Viscountess Beaconsfield. No matter how foolish she appeared in public, Disraeli never criticized her, never rebuked her, and always defended her. His communication was positive, never negative, and theirs was a marriage that worked.[12]

Perhaps you married for love and lately petty arguments, sarcasm, and criticism have been polluting the communication in your home. Make a date this weekend with your spouse and arrange to drive somewhere for dinner. The longer the drive, the better. Take advantage of the time in the car to talk honestly and freely about what has been on your mind. Ask questions like, "What would you do if you could do anything and not fail?" Find out what your spouse's dreams are for your children. Discover his or her greatest joys and disappointments. Kiss in the car, hold hands, and laugh together. Rediscover the person you married through communication.

Learn to speak your partner's love language. What says love to your mate? Is it flowers, an evening out, or candy? Is it helping with the housework or cooking a favorite meal? Perhaps it is something as small as a good-bye kiss or an afternoon phone call just to say "I love you." Learn to speak your partner's love language and speak it often. It is better to invest time now than to spend time and money in a divorce court!

# 10

# What to Do When You're in a Slump

E ven the best of families and marriages will have rough times now and then. Personal and family crises will come and go, and it is during those times that the family simply needs to pull harder. Be willing to work at a solution. Don't quit!

I'm amazed by the quitter's philosophy that has permeated our nation. Kids sign up for Little League and if after two games they don't take to it right away, "Quit!" say their parents. They do.

People take sacred marriage vows and after their first disagreement the husband says, "Well, I guess we were wrong. We are not going to be able to make this work." Says she: "I'll call my lawyer and you call yours." They quit.

Young people who battle loneliness sit in their rooms and sulk about their problems. *Better to take a gun and end it all,* a young man thinks. He simply quits on life, bringing untold heartache to his family and friends.

But quitting is no answer. If your forefathers had quit during the struggles of the war-torn years in American history, you would probably not have the freedoms you enjoy today. If your grandparents had quit during the Depression, you would not be here. If your parents had quit caring for you when you went through those unlovely stages of adolescence, you would not be where you are today.

Gary Carter, a New York Mets All-Star catcher, hit his two hundred ninety-ninth homerun in 1988. The Mets were in first place and it seemed as though nothing would stop Carter from easily hitting his three hundredth homerun. The pressure was on. His team, his family, and his fans waited during each game for number 300.

But for two months, Carter could not hit a homerun no matter how hard he tried. It seemed as though fate was against him. What did he do? He went back to the basics of baseball. He watched game films, took extra batting practice, listened to basic batting instruction from his coaches. Even though he was a pro and had been a *great* player for many years, he knew even he could learn much from reviewing the basic skills of baseball.

In July 1988 he finally hit number 300 and was back on track. In fact, he was an improved ballplayer. What was the secret of his success? Some would say it was his review of the basic skills; others would say it was his willingness to reach for outside help. But the bottom line was that he did not give up; he did not quit.

If your family is in a slump or your marriage in the doldrums, you could profit from a review of the basics and perhaps even from reaching out for help. Getting help from a counselor is not a sign of weakness but a show of willingness to solve problems.

## Seek Help

"The lean times were probably the best thing that ever happened to this marriage," say David and Trudy Burke. "It gave us a chance to say, 'We're really not communicating'."[1]

Many couples cannot agree upon counseling until it is too late. "I asked him to go with me to a counselor for years, and he simply wouldn't admit we had a problem," one wife told me. "Now that I've left him, he's willing to go for help, but it's too late. If he wouldn't work on our marriage while I was there, it's silly to work on it now that I have a life of my own."

Marriage counselors advise husbands and wives to see a counselor alone if their spouse won't join them. Perhaps a husband insists he won't "air his dirty laundry" in front of a stranger. But if the wife begins counseling, often the husband will follow simply out of curiosity—he wants to know what has been said and he would like to tell his part of the story.[2]

Even if your marriage partner flatly refuses to go for counseling, if you receive help, instruction, and a review of the "basics" for marriage, you will learn how to manage at least half of your marriage relationship. As you change and learn to communicate better, your marriage will change too.

## Marital Burnout

The word *burnout* has been tossed back and forth in the business world, and it is being applied to marriages too. In an article entitled "'And They Lived Happily Ever After' Is a Rarity in Marriage," the author states that "true marriage burnout is a state of physical, emotional, and mental exhaustion caused by long-term, emotionally demanding situations in which a discrepancy between expectations and reality exists."[3] Just reading a sentence like that can burn someone out!

Seriously, I believe that marriages "burn out" and fall into "slumps" when people simply do not take the time to maintain the relationship. A marriage is like a garden: it must be watered, fed, weeded, and carefully and lovingly cultivated. If all is done properly, a marriage can bring forth much fruit and beauty.

Choose to make your spouse and your family important. Once when the American novelist Sinclair Lewis was courting Dorothy Thompson, he followed her across Europe and all the way to Moscow. At the Moscow airport the press was waiting to greet him. "What brought you to Russia?" Lewis was asked.

"Dorothy," he said.

"We mean, what's your business here?" the press persisted. "Dorothy."

"You misunderstand. What do you plan to see in Russia?"

"Dorothy," quipped Lewis.[4]

Are you as single-minded in your pursuit of family happiness and success? Are you willing to overcome difficulties and make your marriage and family your first earthly priority?

You must first be willing to clear your life of *chemical addictions*. Did you know that the leading cause of divorce in America is alcohol and drug abuse? Substance abuse and the personality disorders that develop from it destroy more marriages than anything today. Do not succumb to this fatal attraction. I was once a slave to that subculture of humanity, but Jesus met me there and lifted me high above it. All my life I wanted and searched for a real home, and now I have a home and a family far lovelier than anything I ever imagined. It was Jesus Christ who gave me the strength to clean up my life.

The second leading cause of divorce is *adultery*, or as it is commonly know today, unfaithfulness. When a man or woman has an affair outside of marriage, the trust relationship of the marriage is broken, sometimes irretrievably. Adultery is a sin against God and one's mate. But it can be forgiven and your marriage can be mended.

144

The third most common cause for divorce today is *economic pressure*. In these homes both parents are usually employed, and both partners are hard-pressed to meet the needs of family, career, and marriage. The mother works harder than Superman to keep home, house, health, and kids together, and the husband often feels underappreciated and inadequate because his salary alone cannot meet the family's needs. This is an emotional situation, and everyone in the family suffers from the stress and strain.

## Reluctant Commitments

Once a pastor told me about his marriage: "I just don't love her anymore," he said, shrugging his shoulders. "We just don't get along and it's hurting the kids. We may as well hang it up."

Ours is a society long on pleasure and short on commitment. People want whatever makes them feel good, even if it hurts someone else. Jesus said that people get divorced because of the hardness of their hearts (Matt. 19:8). Given this country's rate of divorce, our society must have a lot of hardhearted people. I know that sounds harsh, but I know what divorce can and will do to people. I have seen its awful effects more often than I care to remember.

Your marriage commitment needs to be constant, definite, and constantly reaffirmed. Commitment is like milk—it smells bad if not kept fresh.

I heard about a miserable couple who went for counseling. The wife's chief complaint was that her husband never told her he loved her. "I told you that thirty years ago when we got married," her husband mumbled. "If anything changes, I'll let you know."

But what if two people have simply "fallen out of love?"

145

What if the tingles and excitement just aren't there anymore? Well, folks, I have been married for many years and I can tell you that there are many days when the tingles simply disappear. It is a rare bride or groom who can wake up in the morning, glance over at his or her partner with the mussed hair and bad breath, and feel tingles. But love is more than tingles.

Look at 1 Corinthians 13:4–8 where real love is described:

> Love suffers long and is kind; love does not envy; love does not parade itself, is not puffed up; does not behave rudely, does not seek its own, is not provoked, thinks no evil; does not rejoice in iniquity, but rejoices in the truth; bears all things, believes all things, hopes all things, endures all things. Love never fails.

As I have said before, love is an *action* word. Love trusts, hopes, perseveres, and lasts. But tingles have no staying power.

I like the way Gary Chapman puts it: "How warm do you have to feel to be kind? Must we have the 'tingles' in order to be courteous? Can we be patient toward our mate without a warm feeling? You see, the kind of love described in 1 Corinthians 13 does not emphasize emotion but attitude and action. Attitude and behavior are not beyond our control."[5]

You may not feel like love, but you can act like love. And the beauty of love is that once you start acting it, you will start to feel it. Love is a conscious decision to make someone precious to you.

If you start listening to your partner and being kind, soon you may notice him or her blooming under your loving attention. If you will stop talking long enough to hear what your spouse is really saying, you may find someone who needs respect, encouragement, and love from you. Your spouse wants and needs you to be a cheering section, not a critic.

## Managing the Money

A common problem that drives couples apart is the matter of family finances. "Having enough money for a secure future is now the number one prenuptial fear, according to both survey results and relationship experts," says Julie Vargo-Turi.[6]

Does your family feel stressed because of the way you and your spouse handle money? Usually, one partner is a spender and one is a saver. Ultimately, there is a power struggle.

Author Barbara DeAngelis writes, "While times have changed, our values haven't. Subconsciously, a man still feels he has to make enough money to support his wife, and women still feel that it is not right to make more money than their husbands. We have old values clashing with new realities, which can cause problems."[7]

To prevent dollar dilemmas, experts recommend talking about money with your partner. Determine your family's financial goals, set deadlines, and work together to meet them. Reach a "no questions asked" agreement about how personal disposable income will be handled.[8]

Be realistic. If your wife can make more money than you, let her. If that bothers you, discuss it. Does it bother you because you feel like a failure? Steps can be taken to overcome that feeling. Does it bother you because it goes against your preconceived ideas of what the "breadwinner" should be and do? The two of you need to realign your values with open minds and be ready to compromise.

No one can feel good about a marriage and family where the finances are insecure. If you are between jobs, do something to bring in money. Make an active effort. Discuss your feelings and work together toward a positive attitude. If you are heavily in debt, that debt will nag both of you and be a constant source of irritation and worry.

There are many fine books in print about God's plan for

family finances. They teach how to make a budget and how to plan for long-range financial security. Don't fight about your money hassles, make a financial plan and stick with it. You and your mate will be glad you did.

An older Christian lady recently told me that today too many Christians are ready to *go*, as in the Rapture, but they are not willing to *grow*, as in the here and now. When the going gets rough, they're ready to bail out and leave their troubles (and their marriages) behind, but they are not willing to tackle the problems that could help them grow.

Perhaps you don't want to love your partner because you think he or she is simply unlovely. *You can't understand*, you may think. *I live with this woman and she is nothing like she was when we married!*

You ladies are probably thinking, *Oh, I knew he wasn't perfect when I met him, but I planned to change all that. Now I realize I can't.*

You can love someone who is unlovely; mothers do it all the time. Your kids are not always at their best, but even when they are not you still love them. They are not always kind or polite or appreciative, but you love them in spite of their wrongdoings.

God loves us when we are unlovely. His unconditional love is available for you and your marriage. In Romans 5:5 the Bible tells us that "the love of God has been poured out in our hearts by the Holy Spirit." If you can ask God to forgive your lack of love toward your husband or wife and your family, God will forgive you. Better still, He will fill your heart with His love.

If you choose to love, you will have to make commitments of time, honesty, and sexuality. First, it takes time to love someone. You cannot do the kind things that lovers do if you don't make time for them. Set aside the rush of business and hobby and give your spouse the time it takes to walk around the block together. Go on a picnic with the kids or arrange for an overnight baby-sitter and treat your wife to dinner—and an evening away—in your city's nicest hotel. Take time to talk, time to pray, and time to play. Love takes time.

Love demands honesty. If you lie or pretend in your relationship, you are not achieving true intimacy. Intimacy is honest. There is no room for pretense. Stop spending your time idly wishing "If only we were rich . . . if only I had married someone else . . . if only I hadn't said what I did." People who spend all their time wishing never reach the goals they could reach.

## Sexual Pleasure Can Make a Difference

Your mate wants you to enjoy your sexuality. Many men say their wives are lukewarm or even frigid. "She's the ice lady," one man said of his wife. "She acts like sex is just one big favor she's doing for me."

God designed you as a sexual being. Every part of your body, including your sexual organs, were designed by Him for reproduction and pleasure. Within marriage, physical love is to be celebrated. Read the Song of Solomon together with your mate and watch how the sparks can fly.

Remember that you must be honest and communicate with your mate even about the process of making love. Let your spouse know what pleases you. Too many people assume that men and women naturally know what to do. That is simply not true. Don't be afraid or embarrassed to let your feelings be known.

When was the last time you and your husband ate breakfast together in bed? When was the last time you brought flowers to your wife? How long has it been since you took a walk together and held hands? You and your spouse can make

149

today the last day of your marriage slump and the first day of your new romance.

## For the Kid's Sake

Your family will profit from your renewed marriage relationship too. I have heard it often said that the best thing a father can give his son is a father who loves the boy's mother. That is true, and it works for mothers too. Mothers, the best example you can set for your daughters is to love your husband.

If you can pull your marriage out of a slump, you are well on your way to reviving your family as well. In order to meet the challenges of parenting, spend time in prayer, in Bible study, and consult the expert opinions of people like James Dobson, who has written many excellent books on childrearing and family life.

But the best thing you can do is admit your lack of knowledge. God wants you to depend on Him, not on your understanding or wisdom. Kevin Huggins, a counselor for adolescents, tells the story of Mitch, a father:

> Mitch recently shared with me what he called a startling revelation. "You know, I'm starting to understand at least part of the reason why God has given me the children He has. They're tough kids, but God knew I needed tough kids. Before they came along, I thought I had it made. In regular surgeon-style, I had everything sewn up. So much so that I really did not practically need God. When my kids began to bleed, in a manner of speaking, I went to work to sew them up, too. But nothing I did worked. It was the first time that my mind and my skills were not enough."[9]

Can you thank God for the kids He has given to you? Can

you truly and from a grateful heart thank God for your marriage partner? Do you receive your partner as a gift from God, perfectly designed to meet your needs and challenge your weaknesses? If you can, you are on your way to a new beginning. If you begin each day with a new awareness of each person in your family as God-given gifts, you will never fall into a slump again!

It is through cooperation that people succeed in this life. God works with you; you work with each other. No wonder the Bible says, "Come, let us reason together. . . ." Derric Johnson says it well: "Cooperation is a valid spiritual concept. I do something and God does something and the real successes come as we work on the same things at the same times from different ends. God expects me to do all I can—then He does the rest. I work like everything depends on me—and I pray like everything depends on Him."[10]

Of course, you do not know everything about being the parent and spouse you should be—neither do I! But I know someone who has the answers I need, and I am not shy about asking for His help. His help is available for you too. So go to Him and ask away. He's ready to listen.

# 11

## The Point of No Return:
### *Living with Divorce*

S o far this book has been a shotgun blast that has hit many issues which could affect the lives of millions of Americans who face a splintering family. But what if divorce has already occurred in your home? Your family has already broken into pieces—how can you pick up those pieces and go on? Is it too late for anything other than second-rate survival?

Not many years ago a popular television star was interviewed by Barbara Walters. The glamourous star stated that she considered her second marriage a success. "But didn't it only last three years?" asked Miss Walters. Her question surprised the star. "I consider a marriage of three years a success," she said simply.[1]

No matter how flippant society becomes about divorce and its regular occurence, to most individuals it is still a personal crisis. Love has been lost, vows have been broken, security has vanished. How do you survive the heartbreak of divorce?

If you have gone through a divorce, you must undergo a healing process before you can get on with the rest of your life. No one can stand before you and make the hurt go away and renew the dreams you thought were lost. On your own timetable, you must first heal. You can recover. You can be happy again.

## Take Time to Mourn

But first you need to take the time to mourn over the marriage that once was. During mourning you may go through the typical stages of grief. There are five stages most people go through:

- Denial: "I can't admit I was hurt."
- Anger: "I blame others for hurting and destroying me."
- Bargaining: "I set up conditions to be fulfilled before I'm ready to forgive."
- Depression: "I blame myself for letting hurt destroy me."
- Acceptance: "I look forward to growth from hurt."[2]

If you have been hurt by a divorce, allow yourself whatever time you need and don't feel badly about telling your friends: "Thanks for offering to set me up with a date, but honestly, I'm not ready to begin dating yet."

## The Emotional Stages of Divorce

Jim Smoke, who has worked with single adults for years, says the first emotional state many people go through in a divorce is *shock*. Some people retreat within themselves, refusing to acknowledge their problems or confide in anyone. But "denying the divorce will not make it go away. Hiding it from family and friends will not resolve it."[3]

The second stage of coping with divorce is *adjustment*. "Adjustment," says Smoke, "means that you begin to deal with the reality that this has really happened to you. Shock is accepting the facts of divorce, adjustment is doing something about it."[4]

Adjustment is the putting together of a new lifestyle. Perhaps you face a new apartment, a new job, a new city, or a new church. You definitely face a new situation: you are no longer married, you are single again. You may not be the full-time parent you once were. You may have much more or much less free time than you had when you were married. You are regarded differently by your friends and neighbors. At first, you may not have much liked the changes in your life, but you learned to adjust to them.

The third stage following a divorce is *growth*. "You grow a little each day even if you can't see it or feel it. Good growth happens when conditions are right. Good growth begins when a person says, 'I want to grow and learn from my experiences'."[5]

Smoke gives eight steps for growing through divorce:

1. Realize that time is a healer and you must walk through that process one day at a time. No one can walk through it for you. No one else will have your exact feelings and experiences. Some days the growth time will be an hour or maybe even half of a day. But you will only grow as you walk through the process.

2. Come to grips with yourself. You can't deny your existence no matter how frustrated, lonely, guilty, angry or desperate you may feel.

3. Set aside time for reflection, meditation, reading, thinking, and personal growth. There are many situations around you that you will be powerless to change. But you can always work on changing yourself. Allow yourself some time to do this.

4. Get with healthy people who are struggling but grow-

ing. There is only minimal comfort in hearing other peoples' divorce stories while you are going through yours. At first it may be a help but soon it becomes a bore. Healthy people are those who let the past die and who live and grow in the present.

5. Seek professional counseling or therapy if you feel you need it. Asking for help is a sign of strength, not weakness. Many counseling centers offer divorce recovery workshops that can be invaluable in helping you gain insight into your situation.

6. Accept the fact that you are divorced (or divorcing) and now single. Many divorced people still feel married. A lady summed up her feelings one day by saying that she was not single but merely between marriages. If you are divorced, you are single.

7. Put the past in the past and live in the present.

8. Commit your new way to God, begin new things and seek the help and relationships you need to *begin again*.[6]


## Pride and Anger: Destructive Twins

If you have been divorced, your pride usually must heal first. Since your relationship has openly and publicly failed, your ability and worth as a husband or wife have been called into question. *Everyone is probably wondering what I did to break up my marriage,* you may think. *No one will ever want to be with me again because my reputation is ruined.*

When a person's pride is hurt, the usual and normal reaction is anger. Adults feel it. Children feel it. Divorce arouses anger like nothing else, and the anger is usually focused on the wrong person or thing. Children tend to become angry at one parent or the other; at times they are angry at the entire

155

world. The divorcing partners usually vent their anger on each other. "You hurt me and you deserve to be hurt back," rings the battle cry for vengeance.

A few years ago an "ABC Nightline" featured Scott Fulmer, whose ex-wife kidnapped their son in an effort to get back at him. Taylor Walker, an attorney who once snatched his daughter from his ex-wife, acknowledged that vengeance was his prime reason for child-napping.

These feelings are difficult to expel because memories cannot be erased overnight. In *Living Beyond Divorce*, Jim Smoke writes, "The difference between the death of a mate and the divorce of a mate is that death leaves you with a file of good memories of yesterday while divorce leaves you with a 'ring around the collar' memory of yesterday."[7]

Memories of the past will always remain but they need not destroy the future. You do not have to put your former spouse on a pedestal, but neither do you have to tear him or her down in order to win over your kids. Make sure your anger does not color all of your memories of your ex-spouse. Constant criticism of your ex-spouse will only make your children miserable. Choose what to remember. Remember your ex-spouse's good points and let your children know that there are many things that are admirable about their mother or father. This does not mean you should overlook their faults, some of which may be very serious, but neither do you need to constantly call attention to them. Dr. Avodah K. Offit, a psychiatrist, observes that no one partner bears all the blame for divorce. "The best way to begin to move on successfully to the next phase of life is to take a courageous backward look. This is an essential part of the grieving process."[8]

One of the difficult issues of living with a divorce is the matter of co-custody of children. Once the court's ruling has been given, your problems have only just begun. Arranging visits, vacations, holidays, and travel times around school schedules, baseball practices, field trips, piano lessons, and homework can become difficult and exhausting. You will need to be extremely patient and supportive of one another throughout this process.

Another difficulty with co-custody is the consistent application of rules and standards. Often one parent will become more lenient in an attempt to win favor and acceptance from the child. Many unfortunate and unnecessary conflicts can result at this point. Again, it is the child who is caught in the middle. As difficult as it may be, you need to discuss these matters with each other and come to a common agreement on guidelines for behavior.

## Recapturing the Future

Another common reaction to divorce is an overwhelming feeling of hopelessness. This may set in after the anger has been expelled. *My life is over*, a divorced person may think. *All my years were wasted in that marriage. I'll never be happy again.* If you were a happy person before the divorce, you can be happy again.

You are still a person whom God loves. No matter what unkind or unthinking people may say, you are worth loving! I love the song popularized by Sandi Patti, *In Heaven's Eyes*. It could have been written for you.

> A fervent prayer rose up to heaven
> A fragile soul was losing ground—
> Sorting through the earthly babel,
> Heaven heard the sound.
>
> This was a life of no distinction,
> No successes, only tries.
> But gazing down on this unlovely one,
> There was love in Heaven's eyes.

The orphan child, the wayward father,
The homeless traveler in the rain—
When life goes by and no one bothers,
Heaven feels the pain.

Looking down, God sees each heartache,
Knows each sorrow, hears each cry—
And looking up, we'll see compassion's fire
Ablaze in Heaven's eyes.

In Heaven's eyes there are no losers,
In Heaven's eyes, no hopeless cause.
Only people like you,
With feelings like me—
Amazed by the grace we can find
In Heaven's eyes.

In the eyes of God, my friend, you are not a loser if you know Jesus Christ as Savior. You are a child of the King, and all of His riches and strength are at your disposal. Call upon Him when your days grow long and lean upon His strength. The fruit of His Spirit is love, joy, peace, patience, gentleness, goodness—all the things you need to *grow* through a divorce, not just *go* through one.

## The Children of Divorce

Perhaps the people most wounded in a divorce are the children. As a single parent, how do you cope with the unique pressures you face?

First of all, despite all the facts and figures about troubled kids from broken homes, there is hope. Emmy E. Werner, a social psychologist at the University of California, has studied

698 people born on the Hawaiian island of Kauai in 1955. A third of these people were born into homes marred by poverty, divorce, alcoholism, mental illness, or physical abuse. Most of these children did not break out of the cycle of hardship, but one of four *did*.[9]

How did they do it? It is only speculation to know what makes a child rise above his circumstances, but Werner found it was important for children to have an "opportunity to establish a close bond" with someone. Family stability was also an important factor (children from broken homes fared worse than did children from two-parent families), but those who had consistent loving care fared better than those who were bounced from caretaker to caretaker.[10] As Robert Louis Stevenson said, "Life is not a matter of holding good cards but of playing a poor hand well."[11]

No one would deny that divorce is deeply traumatic for children, but parents can make the trauma easier to bear. "Most people don't divorce well," says Constance Ahrons, an associate director of the Marriage and Family Therapy program at the University of Southern California, "but some parents manage to put aside their anger and put the issues of parenting first."[12]

Parents who place their child-rearing responsibilities aside after the divorce in order to continue an onslaught of bitterness and anger against the ex-spouse will find that their children's wounds never heal but continue to bleed and fester. "Divorce may be a plausible option if it leads to less parental fighting," says Rex Forehand, a family psychologist, "but it is a horrendous option if it does not."[13]

Mike Kachura, a Christian family counselor in Lynchburg, Virginia, says the first thing divorced parents must do is cooperate. "If anything, it is damaging to the children to see their parents continue to 'go for the jugular' and use those children to hurt or try to coax the other spouse back. The children must realize they had no part in the divorce and they are not to blame. The parents must come together and cooperate in child-rearing, and that involves not using the children or communicating through the children, but commanding respect of the other parent through the children. Parents must reaffirm their love and commitment to the child."[14]

Devastated children may reveal their inner turmoil after a divorce in many ways, including truancy, clinging, withdrawal, bed wetting, aggressiveness, nightmares, and poor work at school.[15] Ed Dobson has noted six negative effects of divorce on children:[16]

*Anger.* Recent opinion surveys show that almost all young people experience anger at one or both parents when a divorce occurs.

*Fear.* Many kids fear being forgotten or abandoned by divorcing parents. Others fear the future, which seems bleak and unstable.

*Loss of identity.* Since the self-image of a child is closely related to family structure and development, children of divorce feel a great sense of insecurity and personal loss.

*Loneliness.* Wallerstein and Kelly observed that the children of divorce feel lonely and isolated. They are often "paralyzed by their own conflicting loyalties . . . [thus] many children refrained from choice and felt alone and desolate, with no place to turn for comfort or parenting."[17]

*School performance.* Nearly half of all the children of divorce experience an immediate and noticeable decline in school performance. They seem preoccupied with the conflicts of their parents and the effect of those conflicts on them.

*Parent-child relationships.* While the effects of divorce on the parent-child relationship vary within given families, it has become increasingly clear that many children take sides and reject one or both parents as bad. In most cases one parent influences the child to believe that he or she is right and the other parent is wrong.

Researchers Swihart and Brigham isolated several key factors that lessen or increase the impact of divorce.[18]

---

### Divorce Adjustment Factors

| Lessens Impact | Increases Impact |
|---|---|
| 1. Parents do not put children in the middle. | 1. Children are asked to choose between parents. |
| 2. Children are told about the separation. | 2. Children are not told about the separation or are given little information. |
| 3. Children are aware of the conflict between parents. | 3. Parents hide conflict and anger. |
| 4. Children are not held responsible for the divorce. | 4. Children are made to feel that the divorce is their fault. |
| 5. Children are not used for parental support. | 5. Parent relies on child for personal support. |
| 6. Children receive support from significant people. | 6. Children are isolated from family friends. |
| 7. Parents resolve personal anger. | 7. Parents are unable to resolve anger. |

161

| Lessens Impact | Increases Impact |
|---|---|
| 8. The absent parent stays in contact with the child. | 8. The absent parent has little contact with the child. |
| 9. Siblings. | 9. Only child. |
| 10. Family moves into a new schedule fairly quickly. | 10. Family remains disorganized long after separation. |
| 11. Other environmental factors remain stable. | 11. Life is greatly changed: school, neighborhood, parent's work hours, etc. |
| 12. Each parent frequently spends individual time with each child. | 12. Little individual attention is given to children. |
| 13. Parents assist each child with individual adjustment reactions. | 13. Parents are not aware of individual adjustment reactions. |
| 14. Children are allowed to grieve. | 14. Loss is denied—no grieving is allowed. |
| 15. Family focuses on the positive and the future. | 15. Family focuses on present calamity. |
| 16. Parents had previous good relationship with child. | 16. Child had not previously felt loved or valued by parents. |

From *Helping Children of Divorce* by Judson J. Swihart and Steven L. Brigham (Downers Grove: InterVarsity Press, 1982), 39. Used by permission.

---

If you are suffering the trauma and upheaval that comes from divorce, consider the following advice from Dr. Hindson's book, *The Total Family:*[19]

*Don't blame God for your circumstances.* He is not the author of divorce.

*Don't criticize your divorced partner in front of your children.* Remember, he or she is still their parent.

*Don't condemn yourself for circumstances beyond your control.* "I wish I had done better"; or "If I had said this, he wouldn't have left." These are destructive thoughts that will only create false guilt.

*Don't wish you were someone else.* Your children need *you*!

*Don't speculate endlessly about what might have been if* . . . If your partner has left and remarried, accept things as they are.

*Don't over-spiritualize your problems.* Your kids will see right through saccharine discussions about how you are really satisfied that things worked out the way they did. Don't misquote Romans 8:28.

*Don't excuse yourself either.* It takes two to tangle. Don't put all the blame on your partner. Be honest about the breakup of your marriage; your children need to know the facts (depending upon their age and maturity, of course). One of the major complaints I hear from young people about divorce is, "No one ever told me anything. I couldn't understand why."

*Don't become overly dependent on the wrong people.* While friends are important, don't constantly run to them with your problems; even your most well-meaning friends may give you conflicting advice. Learn to place your greatest dependence on the Lord Himself and look for His guidance through advice from mature Christians.

163

*Don't dominate your kids.* And let me add, don't treat them as your confidante. Your children do not need to have your adult-sized problems dumped on their shoulders. They have enough to do adjusting to the divorce on *their* level.

*Don't worry about the future; trust God.*

## Being a Stepparent

If you have been divorced or have married a divorced person, you may find yourself in the role of stepparent. This role is not easy to fill. Children wonder, "Do I have to obey my stepparent?" Parents are not sure whether to tell their child to obey a new stepparent. Here are some considerations you may wish to share with your stepchildren:

First, God chose parents as those through whom He can best work in the upbringing of children. Children are commanded in the Scriptures to obey their parents, to honor their fathers and mothers. Without this foundation, children will never be able to experience the harmony in relationship with their parents that God intended.

The key word in step-relationships is *attitude*. Children must have a willingness to learn to recognize and submit to authority, whether it is the authority of parents, stepparents, marriage, employment, the government, or schools. Cheerful submission is the fulfillment of God's command: "Likewise you younger people, submit yourselves to your elders. Yes, all of you be submissive to one another, and be clothed with humility, for God resists the proud, but gives grace to the humble" (1 Pet. 5:5).

Perhaps your stepchildren think you do not understand them, but this does not excuse them from the command of obedience. The destiny of their lives lies in the hands of God, and He is working to accomplish His ultimate will for their lives through the authorities He has chosen, including stepparents. Children can never go wrong by obeying God.

When a stepparent says no, children should take the time to find out why. Are the parents concerned about schoolwork? Safety? Reputation? Many young people thrive on the fun of involvement, even church involvement, but their behavior at home shows nothing but a poor and bitter attitude.

One young man was forbidden by his parents to attend a church because it was of a different faith than his family's. After a family meeting, they agreed he would attend their church for three months. If after that time he still wanted to attend his new church, he could. This young man maintained a joyful testimony of obedience, and showed that his personal relationship with Christ had changed his life and attitudes. Three months later, with their blessing, he began membership in his new church. He proved to them and to himself that his desire was sincere and pure.

The question of stepparents may seem difficult to children, but that is primarily because they are resenting the removal of a parent they loved and the replacement of that parent with someone new. Children are under the authority of the parent and stepparent they are currently living with, and this changes only when their residence changes, permanently or temporarily.

Your children or stepchildren can and should make you their best friend. No matter what they go through, you will be the one who will be there through thick and thin. But they will not come to you unless you take steps to reach out to them.

As a stepparent, proceed with caution and love but by all means, *proceed*. Don't expect your stepchildren to "turn on" to you like a light switch. It will take time for them to come to love and respect you. Most important, work out the details

165

of discipline, "house rules," and family responsibilities with both the natural parent and stepparent. It will not work if you have one set of rules and your current spouse has another. It will also be difficult if you and your ex-spouse have conflicting values. Stepparenting is difficult, but it *can* work well when everyone is willing to do what is best for the children's sake.

## The Pain *Can* Be Healed

Divorce has its pain, but it does not have to keep hurting. Time will heal your hurt if you will allow yourself to heal. This does not mean to ignore or dismiss your pain, but you need to deal with it in the light of God's grace. He knows all about your life and its failures. He knows you better than anyone knows you, including yourself. In fact, if you really want to understand yourself, you need to see yourself as He sees you.

First, God sees you as a sinner. He knows that you are basically selfish and self-centered. He can see right through all your excuses and alibis. He knows what really makes you tick. But despite this, He loves you like no one else ever could.

Before you can properly love yourself enough to forgive yourself, you have to be convinced that He loves you. Before you can ever learn to love someone again, you have to be convinced that God can love them through you.

Love is not something to fear because you feel incapable of expressing it. Rather, it is the gift of God, the fruit of His Spirit who lives within each believer (see Gal. 5:22). You can love others because He loves you. You can also love them because He who lives within you loves them through you (see 1 John 4:16). This is one of the great principles of the new life you have in Christ.

Your ability to love and forgive those who hurt you in life is the key to freeing your conscience from the guilt of bitterness of the past. If you have been hurt by a divorce, do not keep on hating. Forgive those who hurt you and reach out to them. They need your forgiveness and love and respect as much as you need theirs.

For many years I could not understand why my parents divorced. I blamed them for not loving me enough to stay together and not loving each other. It was not until I became an adult that I realized what had gone wrong in their marriage. Then I could see the regret in their faces, but their regret was futile. They could not go back and undo what they had done.

As the years went by, my father came to the end of himself. Alcohol had ruined his life, destroyed his marriage and our home, and nearly killed him. My father swallowed his considerable pride and went to see counselors for help. Oh, how I admire him for that! Today he is helping other alcoholics and problem drinkers.

My mother had a turning-point experience and experienced God's love for herself. She knew how rich was the life I had found in Christ. My parents never remarried, but they came to see the harm their divorce had caused and they did everything they could to correct it.

You may feel that your divorce was the end of your life, but it was not and cannot be. If you have children, you must pick yourself up and be the parent you should be. And whether you have children or not, you have a life with unlimited potential. Get up, get on track, and start moving!

## Ten Commandments for Formerly Marrieds

1. Thou shalt not live in thy past.

2. Thou shalt be responsible for thy present and not blame thy past for it.
3. Thou shalt not feel sorry for thyself indefinitely.
4. Thou shalt assume thy end of the blame for thy marriage dissolvement.
5. Thou shalt not try to reconcile thy past and reconstruct thy future by a quick, new marriage.
6. Thou shalt not make thy children the victims of thy past marriage.
7. Thou shalt not spend all thy time trying to convince thy children how terrible and evil their departed parent is.
8. Thou shalt learn all thou can about being a one-parent family and get on with it.
9. Thou shalt ask others for help when thou needest it.
10. Thou shalt ask God for the wisdom to bury yesterday, create today, and plan for tomorrow.[20]

# 12

# Your Marriage:
## *On the Rock or on the Rocks?*

In the Sermon on the Mount (Matt. 7:24–27), Jesus talked about two men who built houses: one on the sand and one on the rock. When the storms came, the house on the sand fell flat while the house on the rock stood firm. The same storms hit both homes, but only one could withstand the onslaught—the one on the rock. Then Jesus likened Himself to the rock and encouraged everyone to build their lives on Him. When people do, they are building on the only Rock which will stand forever—the powerful Son of God.

When I was a boy growing up in Florida, we could always tell when a storm was coming. The clouds would darken, the wind would pick up, the tides would shift, and we would all scurry for cover. But today, while the storm clouds gather, the winds of criticism blow, and the tides of indifference shift, people go right on living for themselves and building their lives on the shifting sands of human opinion.

"But, Jay," you may say, "what difference does it make if the same storms hit us all? Why bother if we all must struggle with life's difficulties?" The answer is that our efforts to build on Christ will result in a home that can withstand life's storms. Without Him as the foundation, our home will collapse under the strain, and "great [will be] the fall of it."

Happily married people are healthier and live longer. And spiritually committed people are happier people. The two go hand in hand: God and marriage.

When you build your home on the right foundation, your family can withstand any storm, but when you build it wrong, it is bound to fall. The foolish man, who built his house on the sand, reminds me of Abraham and his nephew Lot. Their stories are told in the book of Genesis. Both were wealthy and blessed by God, but Lot became selfish and his selfishness destroyed him and his family too.

While the Bible speaks much of Abraham's faith in God, it never mentions anything about Lot's beliefs. Though Abraham built many an altar to worship God, there is no record that Lot ever built an altar. Abraham built an altar and pitched his tent. But Lot built his tent and pitched the altar! Like all foolish men, Lot thought he could do it all himself.

*He was weak in his devotions.* Though he believed in God, he never had any time for God. As a result, his wife became indulgent, his sons-in-law indifferent, and his daughters immoral.

*He was worldly in his desires.* The Bible records that Lot made selfish choices and eventually "pitched his tent toward Sodom." Soon, he moved into that wicked city, and its ungodly influence took its toll on his family.

*He was wrong in his decisions.* Somehow Lot became the victim of his own selfish decisions. Before it was all over, he lost his wife, his children, his home, and his testimony. Today, he is remembered as a failure rather than as a success.

If you really want to make your life and marriage count, let God have control. Do not be afraid to admit you have

170

failed. Turn it all over to Him. Do not let the hurts and wrongs of the past keep you from a wonderful future in Christ. Now is the time to turn to Him and let Him take control of your life. You and your family will never be the same.

Just before my mother passed away in 1980, she asked God's forgiveness for her sins and placed her trust in Christ as her personal Savior. Though she is gone now, I know she is in a far better place than she ever knew here.

As the years have passed, my father and I have been able to communicate about the scars of the past. It has been a thrill to watch him overcome his alcoholism and reach out to others who struggle with the same addiction.

God has done a great work in our family. He can do the same in yours! Let Him take control. You will never regret it.

## Good Partners Make Good Parents

The key concept that runs through this book like a scarlet thread is the fact that good partners make good parents. The more you are willing to work on your relationship as a couple, the better prepared you will be for the challenges of parenting. When things are going wrong in a marriage, they tend to influence and distort everything else in the family.

The more Dad and Mom love each other, the more secure their children will feel. Kids need to be reassured that their little world is not going to fall apart because Mom and Dad are going to split up. The security of a loving and stable family is vital to a child's own stability, success, and maturity.

The more you as a couple are willing to invest in each other, the more you are ultimately investing in the future of your children. Do not make the mistake of putting all your attention on the kids and neglecting each other. The time you spend rekindling the flame of your marriage is ultimately time invested in your children. Becoming a winner at marriage will automatically qualify you to become a winner at parenting. While the two do not necessarily equate, the one is built on the other. If you want to make a significant difference in your family's future, try the following suggestions:

*Put the past in the past.* What's done is done. Stop beating yourself with the club of the past and get on with the present. What you do right now will change your future and that is really all that matters.

*Stop making excuses.* Don't make excuses for what went wrong in your family and don't play the "if only . . ." game. Excuses do not lessen guilt; they only keep the issue alive when it should be buried and forgotten.

*Turn your family over to God.* Confess that you are a confused spouse and parent, and let God handle the things you cannot. Don't worry on your knees, however; learn to pray and leave your concerns in God's hands.

*Rebuild your life and testimony.* No matter how much time it takes, rebuilding is always worth the effort. Rebuild your relationship with your mate and your kids. Rebuild your testimony and reputation in your community. Apologize to people you may have wronged and let them know you are beginning again.

*Don't become easily discouraged.* If you fail again after your new beginning, don't assume you are an impossible case. Don't *quit!* God will see you through. Rebuilding is hard work.

*Stay away from temptation.* Don't go back to the places, habits, and people who set—or kept—you on a wrong course in the beginning. Keep your life and heart morally pure.

*Establish positive goals.* At the end of one week, ask your spouse how you're doing in his or her eyes. At the end of one month, call a family meeting and ask how things have changed and how they can still change for the better.

*Determine that you and your family will be winners through the power of Jesus Christ.* Reach out for others who can help: counselors, church members, Bible teachers, deacons, and pastors. I love the words to this song:

> You say, "Winners don't need a crutch
> Only losers could believe in such"
> You don't need God, you don't need
>     anything
> You'll face life alone
> You take what the future will bring
>
> You think I've missed what success can
>     bring
> I miss success like trees miss cold in spring
> You think that all is far too much to give.
> But that's what Jesus gave
> So that this loser could live
>
> Here's to all the losers
> That lose all guilt and sin
> Here's to life in Jesus
> All of the losers win.

"All the Losers Win," Words by Ed DeGarmo and Dana Key, ©Copyright 1983 Paragon Music Corporation. Used by permission.

Will you and your family be winners? Or will you succumb to the pressures that surround all of us and sadly quit the game?

173

## Your Home: Heaven on Earth

Most of all, fathers and mothers, God has a ministry for you in your home. You may also have a ministry outside your home, but God wants you to first dedicate yourself to the home He has placed within your reach. What greater challenge is there?

If you have children, Scripture admonishes you to perform the following duties of parents:

*Teach* (Deut. 6:7). Teach your children about the things of God when you sit at home, when you walk together, when you gather around the dinner table, and when you put the kids to bed.

*Train* (Prov. 22:6; Deut. 4:9). Train your children as they grow and in ways appropriate to their age level.

*Provide life's necessities* (2 Cor. 12:14). Few parents neglect to provide life's physical requirements such as food and clothing, but how many parents provide the proper emotional and spiritual requirements necessary for a healthy child? Do you give unconditional love, or is a price tag attached to your approval? Does your child understand that he is a spiritual being?

*Nurture* (Col. 3:21). Do not criticize or hopelessly break the spirit of your children, but lovingly bring them up in the training of the Lord.

*Discipline* (1 Tim. 3:4,12). A child with no discipline and no limits knows no boundary of love. Boundaries are important for your child's security. (See also Prov. 13:24; 19:18; 22:15; and 23:13.)

*Love* (Titus 2:4). Few people need to be reminded to love a beautiful baby, but how have you loved your teenager today? Have you spent time with him or her? Have you spoken words of praise, or have you given nothing but nagging reminders? Have you led your child today to an awareness of God?

"See then that you walk circumspectly, not as fools but as wise, redeeming the time, because the days are evil. Therefore do not be unwise, but understand what the will of the Lord is" (Eph. 5:15–17).

How can you establish a happy home in an age when the nuclear, two-parent family seems to be an anachronism? How can you raise teenagers when "adolescence" is practically a social disease? How can you teach your children to be morally pure when the pregnancy rate for American teens is more than twice that of any other industrialized country?[1] How can you honor your marriage vows at work when the boss promises you a promotion for sexual favors?

You can follow God's will and know that He will bless you. Your "Paradise Lost" can become "Paradise Regained." How? Make your home a place of affection, protection, and imitation.

Give your spouse and your children *affection*. Love them and accept them for what they are. Choose a new way to express your love each day. Make a conscious decision each morning: "Today I will love my partner and my kids to the best of my ability."

Make your home a place of *protection*. Relieve stress from your marriage partner by not adding to his or her problems when you meet again after the day's work. Protect your children from influences that would harm them. Know what movies, television programs, and music they are watching or hearing. Do these things honor Christ? Are they beneficial? If not, keep them out of your home.

175

Make your home a place of *imitation*. Children learn by observing their parents, so make your model worthy of emulation. Do you want your children to pick up your habits? Should your children spend their time as you spend yours? If your children treat their marriage partners as you treat your spouse, will their homes be happy?

The chances are great that if you hate carrots, your kids do too! If you like basketball, your kids probably join you for the game in front of the television. If you are indifferent to spiritual things and do not go to church, it is highly likely that your son and daughter will feel the same way.

Coach Price coached the University of California in the 1929 Rose Bowl. On New Year's Day the California team met Georgia Tech on the playing field. Emotions were running high.

On one crucial play there was a fumble, and during the chaos that ensued Roy Riegels of California grabbed the ball and began running *the wrong way*. It took a determined effort for his own bewildered and stunned teammates to bring him down, but they did—just short of a goal. Georgia was quick to turn the gained yardage into a touchdown, and Riegels was not only embarrassed, he was devastated.

In the locker room at half time, everyone expected Coach Price to rant and rave about Riegels' stupid mistake. But the room was deadly silent. Riegels stripped off his jersey and sat sobbing in a corner with a blanket around his shoulders.

When the break was over, Coach Price stood and said simply, "I want the same team that started the game out on the field now." The team stood and ran back out to play—everyone, that is, except Roy Riegels. "Didn't you hear me, Roy?" asked the coach.

"I can't go back out there," said the player. "I've ruined myself, I've ruined the game, I've ruined the college's reputation. I'd rather die than face that crowd again."

Coach Price drew himself up and said sternly, "Boy, the game is only half over. Get out there and play."

California lost that game eight to seven, but those who watched Riegels play during the second half say that they've never seen anyone play football with as much heart.[2]

Be like Roy Riegels and correct your mistakes. Even though you may have been running the wrong way, you can still turn the game around and play your heart out. Riegels could only play on one chilly day in January, but you have an entire lifetime in which to change direction and really love your family.

## For Men Only

I believe the Bible makes clear what roles men are to take in the family. Husband, your wife needs your help. Dads, your children need your leadership. Here are four things you can do that will go a long way toward making your home a better place to live.

*Be a provider.* Most men understand their role as a financial provider but forget that they are to provide not only materially, but also emotionally and spiritually to their family's well-being. Men get their needs satisfied quickly and, therefore, often forget to be sensitive to the needs of their wives and children. You may even have to say *no* to your "toys" in order to better meet your family's needs.

*Be a protector.* Every Mary needs a Joseph. Remember, she rode while he walked. Your wife and children deserve the security of a responsible husband and father who will do whatever is necessary to protect his family from spiritual danger as well as from physical harm. As a spiritual leader in your home, be sure to keep out harmful influences that will pull you away from your commitment to live for Christ.

*Be a priest.* Perhaps as never before, men are needed who are willing to be spiritual leaders in their own homes. Pray with your wife and children. Read the Bible together. Worship God as a family practice in your home. Don't let your wife have to be the one to insist on asking the blessing or reading devotions. You do it!

*Be a pal.* Become your wife's best friend. Remember, the friendship factor is the greatest insulator against divorce. Develop common interests and a strong friendship. Make sure you give plenty of time to your wife in order to grow in your relationship. First Peter 3:7 tells you to *know* your wife, *honor* her, and *share* the grace of life with her. Take time to smell the roses. Life will go better if you do.

## For Women Only

The Bible also clearly prescribes a woman's role in marriage. Women, if you want your husbands to become better leaders, you will have to become better followers.

*Be supportive.* Support his dreams. Don't tell him why he can't, tell him why he can! Treat him like a king and he will treat you like a queen. Become his biggest fan and cheer him on to success. Let him know you are there to help, not hinder. Men often walk out of a marriage claiming they were not appreciated. Give him all the attention and admiration you can.

*Be submissive.* Meet his needs without being asked. Remember, relationships work both ways. The more you follow his leadership, the more he will be willing to lead. If you do not meet his needs, someone else will.

*Be spiritual.* Don't neglect your own spiritual growth. Determine to become more Christ-like in all your attitudes and actions. Learn to be positive and uplifting. Encourage spiritual growth; don't discourage it.

*Be smart.* Keep up with your husband's interests, hobbies, and education. Read and improve yourself. Keep your attractability high. Look sharp, think deep, and develop your full potential in every area of your life.

Remember, marriage is what you make it. The divorce rate just indicates that some are not trying very hard. God can make a difference in your life, and you, in turn, can make a difference in your marriage. And that difference will spell security, high self-worth, and unconditional acceptance, not only to your mate, but to your children as well. They will thrive under the love Mom and Dad show to each other.

What are you waiting for? Help your children answer yes to the questions, Dad, do you love Mom? and Mom, do you love Dad? The first step begins with you.

# Notes

Chapter 1      Paradise Lost: The National Divorce Epidemic

1. Randolph E. Schmid, Associated Press, "One-fourth of U.S. Youth Live in One-Parent Homes," *St. Petersburg Times*, 21 January 1988, 1-A.
2. "A Profile of Tomorrow's Family," *Children Today*, January/February 1985, 8.
3. Arthur J. Norton, "Families and Children in the Year 2000," *Children Today*, July/August 1987, 8.
4. Henry C. Black, ed., *Black's Law Dictionary* (St. Paul: West Publishing Co., 1983), 601.
5. Richard A. Gardner, M.D., *The Parents' Book About Divorce* (New York: Doubleday and Company, 1977), 117.
6. Mike Kachura, personal communication, February 8, 1986.
7. Ann Mitchell, *Children in the Middle: Living Through Divorce* (New York: Tavistock Publications, 1985), 94.
8. Melvin G. Goldzband, M.D., *Easing the Children Through Divorce* (New York: McGraw Hill Book Company, 1985).
9. Susan Grobman, "Child of Divorce," *USA Today*, July 1987, 41.
10. Norton, "Families and Children," 8.
11. Sue Landry, "Educators Say Society Triggers Gun Problems," *St. Petersburg Times*, 28 March 1988, 1-B.
12. Diane Mason, "Married to the Mob," *St. Petersburg Times*, 3 September 1988, 1-D.
13. Andrew Cherlin, quoted in James Dobson's *Focus on the Family*, July 1987, 1.
14. Patricia Nicholas, "Reconciliation, Remarriage: The Trauma Continues," *Psychology Today*, January 1987, 11.

181

15. Sylvia Ann Hewlett, "When a Husband Walks Out," *Parade*, 7 June 1987, 4.
16. "No-Fault Divorce 'an Economic Disaster' for Wives, Children," *U.S. News and World Report*, 4 November 1985, 63.
17. Dr. Armand Nicholi, quoted in James Dobson's *Focus on the Family*, December 1984, 2.
18. Ibid.
19. Lance Morrow, "Through the Eyes of Children," *Time*, 8 August 1988, 33.
20. Dr. Ken Magid and Carole A. McKelvey, *High Risk: Children Without a Conscience* (New York: Bantam Books, 1988), 26.
21. Ibid.
22. Ibid., 183–184.
23. Ibid., 185.
24. Edward Teyber and Charles D. Hoffman, "Missing Fathers," *Psychology Today*, April 1987, 38.
25. Carle C. Zimmerman, *Family and Civilization* (New York: Harper and Brothers, 1947), 776–777.

### Chapter 2     Through the Eyes of Children

1. Barbara Kantrowitz, "How to Stay Married," *Newsweek*, 24 August 1987, 52.
2. "A Grim Picture of Childhood in 1988," *Newsweek*, 6 October 1988, 66.
3. Morrow, "Through the Eyes of Children," 32.
4. William Bennett, from a speech given at Liberty University, Lynchburg, Virginia, April 23, 1986.
5. Morrow, "Through the Eyes of Children," 32.
6. Gerri Hirshey, "What Children Wish Their Parents Knew," *Family Circle*, 8 August 1988, 88.
7. Morrow, "Through the Eyes of Children," 56.
8. Gerri Hirshey, "What Children Wish Their Parents Knew," 85.
9. "Young Children of Divorce: Depressed, Wary, Subdued," *USA Today*, September 1987, 10.
10. Ibid.
11. Phyllis Theroux, "The Meaning of Family," *Parents*, May 1988, 45.
12. Grace Ketterman, M.D., "Raising Children as a Single Parent," *Parents and Children* (Wheaton: Victor Books, 1988), 684.
13. Abigail Wood, "It Was THEIR Divorce. Now It's My Problem!", *Seventeen*, February 1987, 42–43.
14. Dr. Armand Nicholi, quoted in James Dobson's *Focus on the Family* December 1984, 1.
15. Jeff Meer, "Divorce: Do It for the Kids?", *Psychology Today*, July 1987, 21.

16. Gary and Angela Hunt, *Mom and Dad Don't Live Together Anymore* (San Bernardino: Here's Life Publishers, 1989), 75.

## Chapter 3    The Teenage Security Crisis

1. Bonnie Johnson, "A New Study Promises Answers to an Old Question: What's Wrong with Our Kids?", *People*, 15 December 1988, 62.
2. Thomas C. Tobin, "The Year of Living Dangerously," *St. Petersburg Times, Largo/Seminole Edition*, 1 October 1988, 1.
3. John Janeway Conger, *Adolescence and Youth* (New York: Harper and Row, 1977), 246.
4. Ibid., 246–247.
5. "Never a Right Age," *Scientific American*, September 1987, 32.
6. Jennett Conant and Pat Wingert, "You'd Better Sit Down, Kids," *Newsweek*, 24 August 1987, 58.
7. "What Predicts Adolescent Suicide?", *Essentials of Adolescence*, April 1983, 1.
8. Mary Ann O'Roark, "The Alarming Rise in Teenage Suicide," *McCall's*, January 1982, 18.
9. Ibid.
10. Mike King, "Teen Suicide," *Fundamentalist Journal*, April 1988, 27.
11. Associated Press, "Suicide," *Lynchburg News and Daily Advance*, 7 August 1983, 34.
12. "Kids Beating the Odds," *Student Venture News*, Spring/Summer 1988, 1.
13. "Never a Right Age," 32.
14. Susan Grobman, "Child of Divorce," *USA Today*, July 1987, 42.
15. Carin Rubenstein, "The Work and Spend Ethic," *St. Petersburg Times*, 22 January 1988, 1-A.
16. Conant and Wingert, "You'd Better Sit Down, Kids," 58.
17. Johnson, "A New Study," 62.
18. Ibid.
19. Edward Teyber, "Missing Fathers," *Psychology Today*, April 1987, 38.
20. Patricia Nicholas, "Reconciliation, Remarriage: The Trauma Continues," *Psychology Today*, January 1987, 11.
21. Jim Smoke, personal communication, 1988.

## Chapter 4    Teenage Muddles and Marriages

1. Gary and Angela Hunt, *Mom and Dad Don't Live Together Anymore*, 75.
2. Ibid.
3. Joanne Ross Feldmeth, "Child Molestation: Why Good Kids Make Good Victims," *Focus on the Family*, November 1984, 4.

4. Claudia Wallis, "Children Having Children," *Time*, December 9, 1985, 81.
5. Ibid., 78–79.
6. Ibid., 79.
7. Ibid., 84.
8. Magid and McKelvey, *High Risk: Children Without a Conscience*, 270.
9. Brie Quinby, "Teen-Age Mothers: When Children Become Parents," *Family Weekly*, 7 December 1988, 20.
10. Magid and McKelvey, *High Risk*, 117.
11. Ibid.
12. Ibid., 163.
13. Ibid., 162.
14. Ibid., 165.
15. Ibid., 269.
16. Ibid., 171.
17. Ibid., 273.
18. Ibid., 162.
19. Ibid.

### Chapter 5    Fatal Attractions

1. Alan Richardson, "Are Kids Really Drinking More?", *Parents*, 11 April 1989, 21–23.
2. "Teenage Drinking," *USA Today*, February 1988, 3.
3. "Campus Drinking Blues," *Newsweek*, 3 November 1986, 60.
4. Stanley L. Englebardt, "When Your Child Drinks," *Reader's Digest*, November 1986, 110.
5. Ibid., 114.
6. Robert P. Teachout, *Wine: The Biblical Imperative* (Detroit: Richbarry Press, 1987), 10–13.
7. W. Joseph Campbell, "Heavy Drinking a Growing Problem for Colleges," *St. Petersburg Times*, 18 May 1988, 28-A.
8. Anderson Spickard and Barbara R. Thompson, *Dying for a Drink* (Waco: Word Books, 1985), 62.
9. "Teenage Drug Addiction," *USA Today*, 3 October 1984, C-1.
10. Spickard and Thompson, *Dying for a Drink*, 84.
11. Joanne Ross Feldmeth, "Life with an Alcoholic," *Focus on the Family*, February 1986, 12.
12. Family roles outlined by Jane Marks in "The Children of Alcoholics," *Parents*, March 1986, 108.
13. Spickard and Thompson, *Dying for a Drink*, 68.
14. "Alcohol and the Family," *Newsweek*, 18 January 1988, 63.
15. Spickard and Thompson, *Dying for a Drink*, 65.
16. Irving Berlin, *Theatre Arts*, February 1958, 22.

17. "Happiness: How Americans Pursue It," *U.S. News and World Report*, 4 March 1985, 62.
18. John Bartlett, ed., *Familiar Quotations* (Boston: Little, Brown and Co., 1980), 914.
19. Zig Ziglar, *Raising Positive Kids in a Negative World* (Nashville: Oliver Nelson Books, 1985), 41.
20. Dennis Wholey, *The Courage to Change* (Boston: Houghton Mifflin Company, 1984), 21.
21. Earl A. Grollman and Gerri L. Sweder, "Tips for Working Parents—from Kids," *Reader's Digest*, February 1986, 108.
22. Phillip Moffitt, "The Dark Side of Excellence," *Esquire*, December 1985, 44.
23. Quoted by Tom Cunneff, "The Ladder of Success May Lead Only to a High Place to Fall From," *People*, 8 December 1986.
24. "Doctors Say As Many As Six Percent of Americans Obsessed with Sex," *The Washington Post*, 2 November 1988, 86.
25. Steve Dougherty, "Addicted to Love," *People*, 3 October 1988, 125.
26. Ibid., 126.
27. Martin P. Levine and Richard Troiden, "Myth of Sexual Addiction," *Journal of Sex Research*, August 1988, 24–25.
28. Daniel J. Dolesh and Sherelynn Lehman, "Why Affairs Happen," *Reader's Digest*, June 1986, 169.
29. Gregg R. Albers, "Sexual Addiction and Believers," *Fundamentalist Journal*, November 1988, 32.
30. Ibid.
31. William Lee Wilbanks, "The New Obscenity," *Reader's Digest*, December 1988, 23.
32. "Unfaithfully Yours: Adultery in America," *People*, 18 August 1986, 85.
33. Eleanor Hoover, "A Love Doctor Advises the Truth Hurts, But It Also Heals," *People*, 18 August 1986, 94.
34. Warren Bennis and Burt Nanus, *Leaders* (New York: Harper and Row, 1985), 25.
35. J. Allen Peterson, *The Myth of the Greener Grass* (Wheaton: Tyndale House, 1983), 40.
36. Dolesh and Lehman, "Why Affairs Happen," 170.

## Chapter 6    Throw Mama from the Train

1. Clifton Fadiman, *The Little, Brown Book of Anecdotes* (Boston: Little, Brown and Co., 1985), 145.
2. Jeannie Ralston, "Child Support—Getting Tough with Fathers Who Don't Pay," *McCall's*, February 1985, 69.
3. Richard Lacayo, "Second Thoughts About No-Fault," *Time*, 13 January 1986, 55.

 4. Andrew Mollison, "Divorce Reform Has Repercussions," *The Cincinnati Enquirer*, 13 October 1985, 5-F.
 5. Ibid.
 6. Sylvia Ann Hewlett, "When a Husband Walks Out," *Parade Magazine*, 7 June 1987, 4.
 7. "No-Fault Divorce 'an Economic Disaster' for Wives, Children," *U.S. News and World Report*, 63.
 8. Ibid.
 9. Ibid.
10. Hewlett, "When a Husband Walks Out," 4.
11. Brenda Hunter, "The Value of Motherhood," pamphlet published by *Focus on the Family*, 1988, 5.
12. Jim Smoke, personal communication, 1988.
13. Magid and McKelvey, *High Risk: Children Without a Conscience*, 117.
14. Bobbi Williams, "Why Did My Mom Have to Work?", brochure published by Parents of Minnesota, St. Paul, Minnesota.

### Chapter 7    What Is a Family?

 1. Connie Marshner, personal communication, 1988.
 2. Ibid.
 3. Ibid.
 4. Ibid.
 5. Associated Press, "Average U.S. Family Is Smallest Size Ever," *St. Petersburg Times*, 2 June 1988, 1-A.
 6. James Dobson, "Profile of 'Traditional Family' Misleading," *Focus on the Family*, January 1986, 5.
 7. Harry F. Waters, "Overextending the Family," *Newsweek*, 24 November 1986, 78.
 8. Ibid., 77.
 9. Ibid., 78.
10. George Gallup, Jr., *The Search for America's Faith* (Nashville: Abingdon Press, 1980), 44–45.
11. Ed Hindson, *The Total Family* (Wheaton: Tyndale House Publishers, 1980), 10.
12. Nick Stinnett and John DeFrain, "Six Secrets of Strong Families," *Reader's Digest*, November 1987, 132.
13. Dolores Curran, "What Is a Healthy Family?", *Redbook*, June 1985, 88.
14. Stinnett and DeFrain, "Six Secrets," 133.
15. Curran, "Healthy Family," 89.
16. Ibid.
17. Stinnett and DeFrain, "Six Secrets," 133.

18. Gloria Gaither and Shirley Dobson, *Let's Make a Memory* (Waco: Word Books, 1983), 161.
19. Stinnett and DeFrain, "Six Secrets," 133.
20. Paul Lewis, ed., *Dads Only*, May/June 1985, 11.
21. Stinnett and DeFrain, "Six Secrets," 135.
22. Zig Ziglar, *Raising Positive Kids in a Negative World* (Nashville: Oliver Nelson Books, 1985), 89.
23. Gail Sheehy, *Pathfinders* (New York: William Morrow and Co., 1981).
24. Curran, "Healthy Family," 89.
25. Stinnett and DeFrain, "Six Secrets," 135.
26. Ibid.
27. Curran, "Healthy Family," 89.

### Chapter 8    Tamper-Proof Marriages

1. Maria Wilhelm, "Headed for a Painful Breakup?", *People*, 2 March 1987, 43.
2. Ibid.
3. James Dobson, *Love Must Be Tough* (Waco: Word Books, 1983), 30.
4. Mike Mason, *The Mystery of Marriage* (Portland: Multnomah Press, 1985), 105.
5. James Dobson, "Becoming One," *Focus on the Family*, October 1988, 5.
6. Tim and Beverly LaHaye, *The Act of Marriage* (Grand Rapids: Zondervan Publishing House, 1976), 15.
7. Mason, *The Mystery of Marriage*, 134.
8. *Criswell Study Bible* (Nashville: Thomas Nelson, 1979).
9. Tim Timmons, *Communications for Better Living*, October 1984, 5.

### Chapter 9    When Walls Go Up Between Us

1. Vital Statistics Division of the National Center for Health Statistics.
2. See the helpful chapter "On Communication" in *When the Road Gets Rough* by Ed Hindson and Walt Byrd (Old Tappan: Revell, 1988), 33–40.
3. Barbara Kantrowitz, "How to Stay Married," *Newsweek*, 24 August 1987, 58.
4. News America Syndicate, *Reader's Digest*, October 1986, 216.
5. Jim Powers, *Success Is a Family Affair* (Duluth: Parklake Publishers, 1986), 71–72.
6. Michael Zwell, Ph.D., "Are You Listening?", *Brides*, December/January 1979, 49.
7. Angela Elwell Hunt, "Friends in Love," *Fundamentalist Journal*, June 1987, 23.

8. Les Carter, *Push-Pull Marriage* (Grand Rapids: Baker Book House, 1984), 15.
9. Henry N. Ferguson, "Take Out Some Marriage Insurance," *Reader's Digest*, May 1987, 213.
10. Dennis and Barbara Rainey, *Building Your Mate's Self Esteem* (San Bernardino: Here's Life Publishers, 1986), 104.
11. Ed and Carol Neuenschwander, *Two Friends in Love* (Portland: Multnomah Press, 1986), 152.
12. Dale Carnegie, *How to Win Friends and Influence People* (New York: Simon and Schuster, 1964), 82.

**Chapter 10    What to Do When You're in a Slump**

1. Barbara Kantrowitz, "How to Stay Married," *Newsweek*, 24 August 1987, 57.
2. Dianne Hales, "Ten Tips for a Happier Marriage," *Reader's Digest*, November 1986, 166.
3. Mary Jo Kochakian, "'And They Lived Happily Ever After' Is a Rarity in Marriage," *St. Petersburg Times*, 2 October 1988, 7-F.
4. Clifton Fadiman, *The Little, Brown Book of Anecdotes*, 353.
5. Gary Chapman, *Toward a Growing Marriage* (Chicago: Moody Press, 1979), 91.
6. Julie Vargo-Turi, *Dallas Times Herald*, 13 November 1988, 49.
7. Barbara DeAngelis, *How to Make Love All the Time* (New York: Dell Trade Paperback, 1988), 101.
8. Vargo-Turi, 49.
9. Terrence Monmaney, "Kids Who Bounce Back," *Newsweek*, 2 September 1988, 67.
10. Derric Johnson, "Parson to Person," *Regeneration* newsletter, August 1978, 1.

**Chapter 11    The Point of No Return: Living with Divorce**

1. Angela Elwell Hunt, "Surviving a Broken Marriage," *Fundamentalist Journal*, November 1986, 56.
2. Jim Smoke, *Living Beyond Divorce* (Eugene: Harvest House Publishers, 1984), 37.
3. Jim Smoke, *Growing Through Divorce* (Eugene: Harvest House Publishers, 1985), 14.
4. Ibid., 18.
5. Ibid., 21.
6. Ibid., 21–22.
7. Smoke, *Living Beyond Divorce*, 35.
8. Avodah K. Offit, "Surviving a Broken Marriage," *McCall's*, August 1985, 64.

9. Terrence Monmaney, "Kids Who Bounce Back," *Newsweek*, 2 September 1988, 67.
10. Ibid.
11. Ibid.
12. Jennet Conant, "You'd Better Sit Down, Kids," 58.
13. Jeff Meer, "Divorce: Do It for the Kids?", *Psychology Today*, July 1987, 21.
14. Gary and Angela Hunt, *Mom and Dad Don't Live Together Anymore*, 26.
15. Ann Mitchell, *Children in the Middle, Living Through Divorce* (New York: Tavistock Publications, 1985), 62.
16. Edward Dobson, *What the Bible Really Says About Marriage, Divorce and Remarriage* (Old Tappan: Revell, 1986), 106.
17. J. Wallerstein and J. Kelly, "Children and Divorce: A Review," *Social Work*, November 1979, 264.
18. Judson J. Swihart and Steven L. Brigham, *Helping Children of Divorce* (Downers Grove: InterVarsity Press, 1982), 39.
19. Ed Hindson, *The Total Family* (Wheaton: Tyndale House, 1980), 114–115.
20. Smoke, *Growing Through Divorce*, 168.

**Chapter 12      Your Marriage: On the Rock or on the Rocks?**

1. David Hamburg, "A New Study Promises Answers to an Old Question: What's Wrong with Our Kids?", *People*, 15 December 1986, 47.
2. Haddon W. Robinson, *Living God's Will* (Old Tappan: 1976), 16.

## About the Author

Jay Strack is in the ministry to help hurting people. If you have been challenged or convicted by reading this book and want further help, write to him today. If you, too, have a victory testimony to share of how you have been helped by this book, please send it to him. If you would like to volunteer to help others by sharing your testimony, please let us know. You can write to:

Jay Strack
Jay Strack Association
P.O. Box 795337
Dallas, TX 75379